A World Free from Nuclear Weapons

A World Free from Nuclear Weapons

The Vatican Conference on Disarmament

Drew Christiansen, SJ, and Carole Sargent, Editors

Georgetown University Press ✦ Washington, DC

© 2020 Dicastery for Promoting Integral Human Development. All rights reserved. No part of this book may be reproduced or utilized in any form or by any means, electronic or mechanical, including photocopying and recording, or by any information storage and retrieval system, without permission in writing from the publisher.

The publisher is not responsible for third-party websites or their content. URL links were active at time of publication.

Library of Congress Cataloging-in-Publication Data
Names: Christiansen, Drew, editor. | Sargent, Carole, editor.
Title: A World Free from Nuclear Weapons : The Vatican Conference on Disarmament / Drew Christiansen, SJ, and Carole Sargent, editors
Identifiers: LCCN 2019041784 (print) | LCCN 2019041785 (ebook) | ISBN 9781626168039 (hardcover) | ISBN 9781626168046 (paperback) | ISBN 9781626168053 (ebook)
Subjects: LCSH: Nuclear disarmament—Congresses. | Disarmament—Congresses. | Peace—Congresses. | Security, International—Congresses.
Classification: LCC JZ5675 .W67 2020 (print) | LCC JZ5675 (ebook) | DDC 327.1/747—dc23
LC record available at https://lccn.loc.gov/2019041784
LC ebook record available at https://lccn.loc.gov/2019041785

21 20   9 8 7 6 5 4 3 2   First printing

Cover design by Jim Keller.
Interior design by BookComp, Inc.

Contents

Foreword		ix
Cardinal Peter K. A. Turkson		
Introduction: Toward a Positive Peace		xiii
Drew Christiansen, SJ		

Part I: Setting the Agenda

1	Address by His Holiness Pope Francis	3
2	Address by Cardinal Pietro Parolin	6

Part II: Witnesses

3	Surviving the Atomic Bomb	13
	Masako Wada	
4	Hiroshima's Heritage and the Role of Companies in City Reconstruction: How This Experience Shaped Today's Values	16
	Bruno L. Müller	

Part III: Laureates

5	Letter from Nobel Peace Prize Laureates to His Holiness Pope Francis on the Occasion of the International Conference	21
	Mohamed ElBaradei, Mairead Corrigan-Maguire, Adolfo Pérez Esquivel, Jody Williams, and Muhammad Yunus	
6	Nuclear Weapons: Confronting Armageddon	23
	Mohamed ElBaradei	
7	For the Disarmament of Injustice	29
	Adolfo Pérez Esquivel	
8	Will Human Beings Survive Another Century?	38
	Muhammad Yunus	
9	What the International Campaign to Abolish Nuclear Weapons Can Offer for the Future Work of Nongovernmental Organizations	42
	Beatrice Fihn	
10	Nukes, Land Mines, and Killer Robots	44
	Jody Williams	

| 11 | The Peace Process in Northern Ireland
Mairead Corrigan-Maguire | 50 |

Part IV: Diplomats

12	The UN Conference to Negotiate a Legally Binding Instrument to Ban Nuclear Weapons: A Debate Rose Gottemoeller, Thomas Hajnoczi, and Jorge Lomónaco	55
13	Beyond Nuclear Deterrence: Transforming the US-Russian Equation Alexei Georgevich Arbatov	62
14	International Diplomacy and International Security Issues Izumi Nakamitsu	66
15	The Role of International Diplomacy and International Organizations Thomas Stelzer	72

Part V: International Civil Society

16	The Humanitarian Initiative as a Condition for the Ban on Nuclear Weapons François Bugnion	81
17	The Role of Civil Society Susi Snyder	85
18	Reconciliation and Disarmament Marie-Noëlle Koyara	89
19	The Risks of Nuclear War Today Paolo Cotta-Ramusino	97
20	Dealing with Weapons of Mass Destruction in the Middle East Emily Landau	101
21	Nuclear Proliferation in the Middle East: Resolving the Deadlock Ayman Khalil	104

Part VI: More Religious Voices

| 22 | We Must Do No Less
Monsignor Robert W. McElroy | 109 |
| 23 | Transforming the Human Spirit
Hiromasa Ikeda | 113 |

24	Migrations and Wars *Monica Attias*	117
25	The Social and Moral Responsibilities of Knowledge Workers *Drew Christiansen, SJ*	120
26	Preliminary Conclusions *Stephen Colecchi*	135

Part VII: Closing

27	Salutations *Cardinal Peter K. A. Turkson*	141

Afterword: The Holy See and Nuclear Disarmament—Achievements and Challenges   144
Archbishop Silvano M. Tomasi

Contributors   149

Index   153

Foreword

Cardinal Peter K. A. Turkson

Between the winter of 2016 and the spring of 2017, many members and consultors of the former Pontifical Council for Justice and Peace recommended holding a high-level seminar and study session on the issue of disarmament. In hindsight the proposal proved to be a very prescient and discerning reading of the "signs of the times."

We live in a moment of human history when the fear of a potential nuclear catastrophe has intensified to a point rarely experienced before. The global dimension of this catastrophe reminds us of the Cuban Missile Crisis of 1962. Weapons of mass destruction are increasingly being refined for local application and use. New, sophisticated weapons are finding their way into the hands of volatile states and non-state actors. It is increasingly becoming difficult to justify, and to convince people, why some states qualify to own weapons of mass destruction and others do not. The wisdom of Robert Cecil's admonition, "Nations must disarm or perish," inscribed on the portal of the "disarmament room" at the United Nations in Geneva, goes unheeded.[1] Neither have the admonitions of the bishops of the United States—that nuclear armament is never an appropriate policy that constructs a long-term basis for peace, and that the threat of war cannot be reduced with the possession of armaments—made any impact on national and international defense policies. Indeed, global efforts to stop the threat of a nuclear holocaust do not seem capable of leading the world to and along new global pathways of peace.

This growing fragilization of international security and the frantic recourse to stockpiling arms also has a very high economic cost. In his "Chance for Peace" address—delivered shortly after the death of Soviet leader Joseph Stalin—former president of the United States Dwight Eisenhower, a five-star general of World War II, presented an alarming analysis of military spending:

> Every gun that is made, every warship launched, every rocket fired signifies, in the final sense, a theft from those who hunger and are not fed, those who are cold and are not clothed. This world in arms is not spending money alone. It is spending the sweat of its laborers, the genius of its scientists, the hopes of its children. The cost of one modern heavy bomber is this: a modern brick school in more than 30 cities. It is two electric power plants, each serving a town of 60,000 population. It is two fine, fully equipped hospitals. It is some 50 miles of concrete highway. We pay for a single fighter plane with a half million

bushels of wheat. We pay for a single destroyer with new homes that could have housed more than 8,000 people. . . . This is not a way of life at all, in any true sense. Under the cloud of threatening war, it is humanity hanging from a cross of iron. . . . Is there no other way the world may live? (April 16, 1953)[2]

The economic cost of armaments to nations has not decreased. It is, rather, on the rise. And as nuclear power states brace themselves to modernize their nuclear weaponry, one should expect the budget for such upgrades to exceed a trillion dollars. How scandalously huge has this "theft from those who hunger and are not fed, those who are cold and are not clothed" become!

Nevertheless, as Pope Francis noted when he addressed the participants of the Symposium whose papers are published in this book, "a healthy realism continues to shine a light of hope on our unruly world." An instance of this "light of hope" was when a "humanitarian initiative," sponsored by an alliance among civil society, states, international organizations, churches, academics, and groups of experts, got the United Nations General Assembly to approve the Treaty on the Prohibition of Nuclear Weapons in July of 2017. At this UN General Assembly, the majority of the international community recognized not only that these instruments are immoral but that they must also be considered an illegal means of warfare. This decision filled a significant juridical lacuna, for unlike chemical weapons, biological weapons, antipersonnel mines, and cluster bombs, nuclear weapons were not comprehensively prohibited by a specific international convention.

Another "light of hope" was when the International Campaign to Abolish Nuclear Weapons (ICAN) was awarded the Nobel Peace Prize in October of 2017. This award recognized ICAN's role in shedding light on the catastrophic consequences of the use of nuclear weapons, and for its huge campaign in support of the UN approval and adoption of the Treaty on the Prohibition of Nuclear Weapons.

Still another "light of hope" is the UN secretary-general's announcement, a year ago, of his "Securing our Common Future: An Agenda for Disarmament" (May 24, 2018). The agenda outlines a set of practical measures to promote disarmament in the areas of weapons of mass destruction and conventional arms, and to discourage the development of weapon technologies for the future.

Finally, the concept of humanitarian disarmament, which is spearheaded by civil society groups with membership spanning the globe, can also be considered a light of hope insofar as it focuses on preventing and remediating human suffering and environmental harm, rather than on advancing national security.

To contribute to this disarmament momentum, the Dicastery for Promoting Integral Human Development proposes to frame the dialogue on disarmament within the broader context of peacebuilding. This comprises the concept of integral disarmament, which, as explained by Saint Pope John XXIII, does not only refer to state armaments.[3] Rather it calls on every person to disarm his or her own heart and to be a peacemaker everywhere. In this regard, Pope Francis never ceases to emphasize the need for accompaniment and discernment in order to explore alternative courses of action while exercising in-depth moral responsibility.

This is what this book aims to achieve, namely, a *vademecum* on integral disarmament for peace for individuals, communities, and states.[4] Integral disarmament can move us to transform a culture of injustice and violence to a culture of fraternal love and peace, because it takes us beyond peace conventions and treaties to personal and communal conversion and change of heart. Integral disarmament takes us beyond the mentality of finding security only in armament and the preparedness for war, and nurtures a civilization of love and political friendships for the development of the whole person and for all peoples:a development that cares deeply about God's creation in its totality.[5]

I wish to express my sincere gratitude to all those who have contributed to this symposium, and whose addresses make up this volume. Without their efforts, none of this would have been possible. It will take too many pages to mention them all. But I would like single out for a special expression of gratitude Father Drew Christiansen, SJ, for his tireless effort in coordinating the editorial work of this volume over the past two years, and Archbishop Silvano Maria Tomasi, for his wholehearted support in organizing the Symposium that gave birth to this book.

Notes

1. Lord Robert Cecil, 1865–1958, an architect of the League of Nations and a Nobel laureate in 1957.
2. The full text is available at dwighteisenhower.com.
3. Cf. *Pacem in terris*, §113.
4. *Vademecum*, "A book or manual suitable for carrying about with one for ready reference," *Oxford English Dictionary*.
5. Cf. *Populorum progressio*, §14; and *Laudato si'*, §14, 42.

Introduction: Toward a Positive Peace

Drew Christiansen, SJ

Ever since Pope Saint John XXIII, in the wake of the Cuban Missile Crisis, issued his encyclical *Pacem in terris* in 1963, the Catholic Church has been working for a world free of nuclear weapons. Pope John wrote, "Though the monstrous power of modern weapons acts as a deterrent, there is nonetheless reason to fear that the mere continuance of nuclear tests, undertaken with war in mind, can seriously jeopardize various kinds of life on earth."[1] Two years later the Second Vatican Council, contemplating the prospects of nuclear war, urged the world to examine the issues "of war with an entirely new attitude."[2] "Whatever may be the case with deterrence," they pleaded, "the arms race in which so many states are engaged is not a safe way to preserve a sure and authentic peace."[3]

The Evolving Moral Evaluation of Nuclear Deterrence

In 1982, in a speech before the UN General Assembly, Pope Saint John Paul II allowed, in the context of the Cold War, for a conditional acceptance of nuclear deterrence. The following year the US bishops, in their pastoral letter *The Challenge of Peace*, stipulated three conditions to be satisfied for a nation's deterrent to be morally acceptable. In 2017, with the Cold War consigned to history and nine nations employing nuclear arsenals, Pope Francis condemned the threat to use nuclear weapons and their very possession, thereby delegitimating deterrence policy.

Morally Conditioned Acceptance of Deterrence

From the time of John XXIII, the Church has put deterrence in question. But a generation later, Pope John Paul II concluded that "deterrence ... as a step on the way to progressive disarmament may still be judged as morally acceptable," even though it is "always susceptible to the real danger of explosion."[4] The following year, in their pastoral letter *The Challenge of Peace: God's Promise and Our Response*, the US bishops elaborated on this "strictly conditioned" assessment of deterrence, specifying three conditions: (1) the *sole purpose* of possessing nuclear weapons is *to deter* their use by others; (2) arsenals should be *limited to a level sufficient to deter* (and not aim at nuclear superiority); and (3) deterrence should serve as a *step toward progressive disarmament*.[5]

Six years later, in 1989, the Cold War came to an end. In the interim, the Reagan administration and the Gorbachev government in the Soviet Union, with two major arms control agreements, had set in motion significant movement toward arms reduction.[6] As these agreements reduced nuclear arms on both sides, both the Holy See and the US bishops began to call for abolition as the eventual goal of nuclear weapons policy.[7] A decade later the Vatican began voicing its critique of deterrence as an obstacle to disarmament.

At the High-Level Meeting at the United Nations in September 2013, Archbishop Dominique Mamberti, the Vatican foreign minister, declared, "The chief obstacle to starting this work [of phased and verifiable disarmament] is continued adherence to the doctrine of nuclear deterrence." He continued, "Military doctrines based on nuclear arms, as instrument of security and defence of an élite group, in a show of power and supremacy, retard and jeopardize the process of nuclear disarmament and non-proliferation."[8] With Mamberti's address, the Church had dropped the conditional acceptance of deterrence first articulated by Pope John Paul II thirty years before.

The Humanitarian Consequences Movement

That same year the Holy See joined representatives of civil society and nonnuclear states in a two-year series of conferences on the Humanitarian Impacts of Nuclear Weapons.[9] Pope Francis sent a supportive message to the conference, and Archbishop Silvano Tomasi, the papal representative to the UN Disarmament Commission in Geneva, asked the delegates, "Is it not urgent to revisit in a transparent manner, how States, especially nuclear weapon states, define their national security?" He added, "The Holy See continues to question the ethical basis to the so-called doctrine of nuclear deterrence. . . . An ethics based on the threat and mutual assured destruction is not worthy for future generations."[10]

At the same conference, the Holy See released a study paper, "Nuclear Disarmament: Time for Abolition," which offered the most extensive ethical issues of the factors that underpin the moral case for nuclear disarmament and scrutinized the counterargument for the belief that nuclear deterrence is "a stable basis for peace."[11] It contended boldly that "a strategy of nuclear deterrence has created a less secure world. In a multipolar world, the concept of nuclear deterrence works less as a stabilizing force and more as an incentive for countries to break out of the non-proliferation regime and develop nuclear arsenals of their own."[12] Of particular significance was its assessment of the inequality between nuclear and nonnuclear states brought about by the Nuclear Non-Proliferation Treaty (NPT). "What was intended to be a temporary state of affairs," it complained, "now appears to have become a permanent reality, establishing a class structure within the international system between possessing and non-possessing states."[13]

Nonnuclear states, the study paper argued, were liable to intimidation or domination by nuclear weapon states. Think of the Russian seizure of Crimea and its fomenting of secession in the Donetsk region of Ukraine. Under such circumstances, the paper argued, "efforts to enforce nonproliferation give rise to suspicions that the NPT is an instrument of an irremediably unequal world order."[14]

With uncharacteristic irony, the Vatican study text commented, "Non-possession begins to appear inconsistent with the sovereign equality of nations and the inherent right of states to security and self-defense."[15] In addition to the inequality of states and the instability of the NPT regime, "Time for Abolition" appealed to the injury done the global common good and the price nuclear armaments imposed on the poor as reasons to call for prohibiting nuclear weapons.

Abolition

With this thinking in the background, the Holy See joined the UN process leading the 2017 conference that drafted the Treaty to Prohibit Nuclear Weapons.[16] For the first time, the Holy See was seated as a full state member of a UN conference, not just an observer member, and cast its first vote in favor of the treaty. The Holy See was among the first states to sign the treaty and to ratify the Treaty to Prohibit Nuclear Weapons in September of that year.[17]

Article 1 of the treaty commits the signatories not to "develop, test, produce, manufacture, otherwise acquire, possess or stockpile nuclear weapons or other nuclear explosive devices." Furthermore, in an explicit prohibition of deterrence, it forbids the "use or [threat] to use nuclear weapons or other nuclear explosive devices."

The stage was set for Pope Francis's public condemnation of deterrence the next fall. On November 10 and 11, 2017, the Vatican Dicastery for Promoting Integral Human Development, led by Cardinal Peter Turkson of Ghana, convened an international symposium, "Perspectives for a World Free of Nuclear Weapons and for Integral Disarmament." The participants consisted of Nobel Peace laureates, diplomats, and civil society representatives who had participated in the Humanitarian Consequences conferences and the subsequent UN negotiations leading to the Treaty on the Prohibition of Nuclear Weapons in the spring and summer of 2017. Speaking to the participants in that meeting, Pope Francis delivered his public condemnation of nuclear deterrence.

After noting the misallocation of resources from educational, ecological, health care, and human rights goals to the production and maintenance of nuclear arsenals, "the catastrophic humanitarian and environmental effects of any employment of nuclear devices," he concluded, *"the threat of their use, as well as their very possession, is to be firmly condemned"* (emphasis added). Like his predecessors, Pope Francis affirmed that nuclear weapons serve "a mentality of fear" and "create nothing but a false sense of security."

Referring to the last phrase in the conference title, "for Integral Disarmament," he concluded, quoting Pope Saint John XXIII, "Unless this process of disarmament be thoroughgoing and complete, and reach men's very souls, it is impossible to stop the arms race, or to reduce armaments, or—and this is the main thing—ultimately to abolish them entirely" (*Pacem in terris*, April 11, 1963).

Receiving the Condemnation

Many people are wondering what the condemnation of deterrence means for those with responsibilities for national defense. Must they withdraw or resign from participation in nuclear forces? Must scientists and weapons designers find other work? Should policymakers develop alternative policies? What should pastors, ethicists, and pastoral counselors advise those who come to them for guidance?

Moral theologians, political scientists, and veteran policymakers are at work preparing guidance on how Catholics and men and women of goodwill can respond to the Holy Father's judgment. In the meantime, there are four main points, especially for Catholics, to bear in mind when encountering those who question or resist the papal condemnation.

First, Pope Francis is not alone in staking out a position against nuclear deterrence. In adopting the Treaty to Prohibit Nuclear Weapons in 2017, 122 nations voted in favor of a policy of abolition. In addition, senior American statesmen—led by George P. Shultz and including Henry Kissinger, both former secretaries of state—have recognized that shifts in global strategic conditions demand abolition, and so have advocated a global-zero policy for more than a decade. As many as twenty-five years ago, after the end of the Cold War, the US bishops in their pastoral "The Harvest of Justice Is Sown in Peace" had already proposed that abolition should be a goal of US policy. It would be sad indeed to see pastors step back from that position. Abolition is a sign of the times. Pope Francis is not breaking new ground with his condemnation. He is calling the world to meet a crisis on which action is long overdue.

Second, the rejection of nuclear war fighting is at the heart of Vatican II's call for a reevaluation of war "with an entirely new attitude."[18] With the end of the Cold War, the burden of moral examination has passed from nuclear war fighting to the abuses of the strategy of deterrence. Although the Second Vatican Council and Pope John Paul II allowed for a conditional acceptance of deterrence, under Pope Benedict, papal diplomats had already questioned the moral status of deterrence. Pope Francis's condemnation is the necessary next step in this trajectory.

The balance of force between the superpowers no longer defines the global strategic situation. There are now nine nuclear powers, and only five are members of the NPT. In addition, the declared nuclear strategies of the two superpowers no longer restrict the use of nuclear weapons to deterrence, but extend them to defense against nonnuclear threats, a development clearly opposed by the US bishops in their 1983 pastoral letter *The Challenge of Peace*. Modernization programs are building flexible weapons that increase the risks for use of nuclear weapons, do away with the threshold of conventional and nuclear weapons, and lower the bar to all-out nuclear war. Under these conditions, abolition has become an urgent practical imperative to defend humanity's common future.

Third, some are even returning to the preconciliar, pre-Nuremberg argument that those in a chain of command are obligated to obey their superiors. The Second Vatican Council condemned blind obedience to illegal orders as a defense for participation in atrocities, and offered "supreme commendation" for "the courage of those who openly and fearlessly resist" such commands.[19] In 2018 two chiefs of the US Strategic Air Command publicly testified that they would have to resist illegal orders and offer alternative courses of action to their civilian superiors.

Fourth, under Article VI of the NPT, the state parties are required to work for nuclear disarmament in the context of "general and complete disarmament"—a high demand, no doubt. But instead of working to meet this demand, the nuclear-weapons-possessing states have largely ignored this provision, while they have rigorously applied the NPT's nonproliferation provisions selectively against some states and not others. This two-faced policy has undermined the credibility of the NPT.

In sum, by condemning the possession and threat to use nuclear weapons, Pope Francis has lent his voice to an emerging global consensus for abolition. He has built on the teaching of Vatican II and later Church teaching and added to the impetus of international law toward abolition. His is a distinctive voice, but he is not alone.

Finally, older, legalist models of moral theology have left the impression that condemnation means "Stop what you are doing now!" But Pope Francis offers a less narrow, nonapodictic style of moral deliberation. His is a method of accompaniment and discernment. It is the antithesis of blind obedience. It entails (self-)education, accompaniment by a spiritual adviser, prayer, discernment, and exploration of and deliberation on alternative courses of action for responding to the call of conscience. It is a mature exercise in moral responsibility and is the farthest thing from determining the least I can do to avoid sin. It is open to the appeal of the greater good. It marks "the progress of a soul" in response to God's grace. There may be no one answer to the moral offense of current deterrence policy. There will be many ways to fulfill the demands of conscience.[20] The question is not what must everyone do, but rather what must I do, in my circumstances, with my possibilities and my talents?

Looking Ahead

The papers collected in this volume represent the views of members of the humanitarian consequences and nuclear abolition movements, as well as some critics, who participated in a Vatican conference hosted by Cardinal Peter Turkson and the Dicastery for Promoting Integral Human Development on November 10–11, 2017. They include—in addition to Church leaders, Nobel Peace Prize laureates, diplomats, and representatives of international organizations—leaders in international civil society and other religious voices.

Setting the Agenda

We begin with Cardinal Turkson's foreword, where he announces the good news that the global will exists for nuclear weapon states to reduce and eventually eliminate their weapons. Proliferation, he contends, decreases human security and reduces nations' ability to invest in health, job creation, care of the environment, or other factors conducive to long-term peace. A shift toward these elements of peace will establish conditions for true security.

This foreword prepares us for chapter 1, Pope Francis's historic statement condemning nuclear deterrence: "If we also take into account the risk of an accidental detonation as a result of error of any kind, the threat of their use, as well as their very possession, is to be firmly condemned."[21] Responding to an understandable pessimism that abolition will ever be possible, the Holy Father notes how useless, from a tactical standpoint, nuclear weapons are, and he calls for a "healthy realism" to address the utter immorality of the current situation.

In chapter 2 Cardinal Pietro Parolin, the Holy See's secretary of state, recommends extending the concept of "integral ecology" from Pope Francis's environmental encyclical *Laudato si'* to the field of disarmament. "Integral disarmament," as the Holy See uses the term, promotes nuclear disarmament, following the Article VI of the NPT with "general and complete disarmament," at the same time that it entails a transformation of attitudes in international affairs from mutual suspicion to mutual trust.

Witnesses

Perhaps the most moving speech of the symposium was given by Masako Wada, assistant secretary-general of the Japan Confederation of A- and H-Bomb Sufferers Organizations; this appears here as chapter 3. Wada shared what it is to live as a hibakusha, that is, a survivor of one of the two atomic bombs dropped on Japan when she was just two years old.

For more than a century, Hiroshima has been the hometown of the Mazda automobile company, which gave that company a special role to play after 1945 in the city's reconstruction. In chapter 4, Bruno L. Müller, vice president of human resources at Mazda Motor Europe and a one-time resident of the city, recalls how he witnessed firsthand the next generation of a city that rebuilt itself and how it led to Mazda's current push for world peace.

Laureates

Mohamed ElBaradei, the director general emeritus of the International Atomic Energy Agency, with years of experience in preventing the spread of nuclear weapons, observed that whether international security has been based on balance of power or on collective security, the world has failed to establish a stable peace. In the current "absurd and contradictory" geopolitical environment, he notes in chapter 6, the risk of a nuclear conflagration grows all the greater. "We are facing an outright crisis of governance," ElBaradei says, "governments which pursue short-term myopic policies, both informed and hamstrung by party politics, fail to cope with people's expectations or meet new long-term global challenges." Against this background, he opines, "The reliance on nuclear weapons as the centerpiece of our collective security system is horrifying."

The veteran disarmament expert deplores rejection by the nuclear weapon states and their allies of the Treaty to Prohibit Nuclear Weapons. He contends that at the very least, they should embrace the recommendation of the Nobel Prize Committee to "initiate serious negotiations with a view to the gradual, balanced, and carefully monitored elimination" of nuclear weapons rather than cling to a rejectionist stance. He concludes with "the hope that that the views of the weapon states will evolve . . . over time."

In chapter 7, the Argentine Adolfo Pérez Esquivel takes the side of the poor, citing the burden nuclear weapons budgets exact from programs for the poor, a constant part in the Holy See's objections to nuclear weapons systems. Esquivel points out that "money from the war industry does not contribute to development or the redistribution of income." He adds, "By reinforcing this inequity we are complicit in injustice."

Likewise, Muhammad Yunus, the founder of the Grameen Bank, calls in chapter 8 for the world to "redesign our existing unsustainable economic system putting our human values of empathy, sharing, and caring, at the center of all our activities—economic, political and social."

Beatrice Fihn, the executive director of the International Campaign to Abolish Nuclear Weapons (ICAN), asks in chapter 9, "How can never-ending escalation assure peace?" Noting that arms buildup is often the posturing of men, she calls on women to continue their roles as "fierce advocates of disarmament."

Jody Williams, a leader in the campaign to ban antipersonnel land mines, adopts a straight-talk style to address the insanity of nuclear weapons in chapter 10. She points out that they are not inevitable, and we can ban them just as we have previously banned chemical weapons and other unacceptable things.

In her turn, Mairead Corrigan-Maguire, the Northern Irish peace activist, speaking from her personal experience of violence, passionately appeals in chapter 11 for the Catholic Church to discard just war theory, and pleads for a new theory of peace and nonviolence.

Together, the laureates have written to Pope Francis in conjunction with the symposium; see chapter 5. They note that the Church's collaboration with nonnuclear states, civil society, and international organizations had made possible progress toward abolition with the 2017 Treaty to Prohibit Nuclear Weapons. "We must build an inclusive and equitable international security system," they write, "in which no country feels the need to rely on nuclear weapons." Looking to the future they also urge the ban of autonomous weapons. "The best solution to this impending third revolution in warfare," they contend, "is to preemptively ban such weapons before they appear on the battlefield."

Diplomats

At the symposium, a special event was billed as "a debate" about the Treaty to Prohibit Nuclear Weapons between two ambassadors who played key roles in the adoption of the treaty the previous July, Jorge Lomónaco of Mexico and Thomas

Hajnoczi of Austria, with Rose Gottemoeller (United States), the deputy secretary-general of NATO—see chapter 12.

Jorge Lomónaco, currently the Mexican ambassador to the Organization of American States and formerly permanent representative of Mexico to the United Nations in Geneva, describes disarmament as a jigsaw puzzle, with the new Ban Treaty as only one key piece. Other pieces include: the Comprehensive Nuclear Test Ban Treaty and the Fissile Material Cut-Off Treaty; they will also require an elimination system, a verification mechanism, and more to assure a good result.

Ambassador Thomas Hajnoczi, permanent representative of Austria to the United Nations in Geneva, explains Austria's efforts to convince nuclear-weapons-possessing states to sign the UN Treaty on the Prohibition of Nuclear Weapons.

Rose Gottemoeller, NATO's deputy secretary-general, places global disarmament at the center of the work of the North Atlantic Council, the policymaking body of the North Atlantic Alliance. She names two key steps: (1) understanding the conflicts that compel nations to obtain nuclear weapons, and (2) focusing more on disarmament conversations between the United States and Russia.

In chapter 13 Alexei Georgevich Arbatov, head of the Center for International Security at the Institute of World Economy and International Relations (Russia), and Russia's foremost arms control expert, asks whether nuclear weapons possession has really prevented World War III, as some claim. He argues that weapons cannot prevent regional and global war in future decades. He then lays out a comprehensive agenda for renewed negotiation by the nuclear-weapons-possessing states.

In chapter 14 Izumi Nakamitsu, the UN high representative for disarmament affairs in Japan, breaks disarmament into three aspects: international security, citing the "growing illicit arms trade that fuels civil wars, violent extremism, and criminal violence"; conflict resolution, including the nuclear crisis in Northeast Asia; and international security and nonproliferation diplomacy, especially the "dark side of innovation."

In chapter 15 Thomas Stelzer, ambassador of Austria to Portugal, speaks from the heart about how most of the crisis in the world today arises from the building of walls. Using the example of an opera by the Italian composer Luciano Berio, with its singers behind a wall that vanishes, he helps us imagine something similar politically.

International Civil Society

In chapter 16 François Bugnion, of the International Committee of the Red Cross, frames its position in terms of the suffering of the victims of the atomic bombing of Hiroshima. Just as, from the outset, the International Committee called for abolition, so it now promotes the July 2017 Treaty to Prohibit Nuclear Weapons as "an essential and long-awaited step" to a nonnuclear peace.

In chapter 17 Susi Snyder, the nuclear disarmament program manager for PAX, positions civil society itself as an actor in nuclear disarmament. Through every action that is mobilized, every process that becomes more transparent and open, and every atrocity such as Hiroshima that is condemned, civil society has been involved in the campaign for nuclear abolition. Civil society, she argues, is the "public square where we debate our fundamental values and explore how they should shape the institutions of our common life."

In chapter 18 Marie-Noëlle Koyara, minister of state for defense of the Central African Republic, offers her own country as an example of a large African state surrounded by others in crisis. The Central African Republic, she believes, suffers because of the challenges its neighbors face. In the future, she envisages complete disarmament and redeployment of the army in the field for peacekeeping.

In chapter 19 Paolo Cotta-Ramusino, secretary-general of the Pugwash Conferences on Science and World Affairs, which won the 1995 Nobel Peace Prize, points out the long history of errors, miscalculations, and misunderstandings in the deployment of nuclear weapons that have almost brought the world to the brink of destruction. Nuclear weapons policy is all too fallible, permeated by very human motivation, including the global prestige of ownership for smaller nations.

In chapter 20 Emily Landau, senior research fellow at the Institute for National Security Studies and head of the Arms Control and Regional Security Program in Israel, argues that states and their policies, not the weapons they possess, determine peace, and she notes that the established nuclear states have set the rules by which others must play while the proliferators feel free to breach the rules.

In chapter 21 Ayman Khalil, director of the Arab Institute for Security Studies in Jordan, discusses the special importance of the Middle East for nonproliferation conversations. Emphasizing the challenges encountered in attempts to establish a Middle East nuclear weapons free zone, he also discusses issues emerging from the Joint Plan of Action agreement curbing the Iranian nuclear program and Israel's undeclared nuclear arsenal, among others.

More Religious Voices

In chapter 22 Monsignor Robert W. McElroy, the Roman Catholic bishop of San Diego, calls for three conversions in pursuit of a nonnuclear peace: (1) to the perspective of an integrated international common good; (2) from the illusion of safety to the reality of nuclear instability and proliferation, and (3) to the construction of tools of peace.

In chapter 23 Hiromasa Ikeda, vice president of Soka Gakkai International, a Japanese religious nongovernmental organization, notes with optimism that the human spirit can be transformed, and that it is mutable, not fixed, and therefore capable of enacting positive change. Through a Buddhist approach to destructive human impulses, he argues, we "can develop the best qualities inherent in the human spirit."

In chapter 24 Monica Attias, a member of the Community of Sant'Egidio, a Catholic lay movement based in Rome known for its peacemaking and care for migrants and refugees, shares how war leads to forced displacement. She makes a special plea for humanitarian corridors of safe passage for the victims of armed conflict.

In chapter 25, my own contribution aims to model how ethicists and professional groups engaged with nuclear weapons production, deployment, and policymaking might respond to Pope Francis's condemnation of deterrence. I make eight recommendations for role responsibilities of knowledge workers in the nuclear weapons field, particularly the just war analysts who teach others how to think about the ethics of war and peace.

Stephen Colecchi, in chapter 26, titled "Preliminary Conclusions," calls for rigorous verification and compliance measures, global cooperation, and collaboration between the Church, religious communities, civil society, international organizations, and governments.

Closing

In chapter 27, Cardinal Peter Turkson's closing salutations to participants in the Vatican conference, the conference host reiterates the statement of Pope Francis, "Everything is connected," reminding us of the links between development, disarmament, and peace. He asserts that in a mutlipolar world, nuclear weapons fail to provide security, and he pleads for more states to sign and ratify the Treaty on the Prohibition of Nuclear Weapons.

Archbishop Silvano Tomasi has been Pope Francis's point person on nuclear disarmament. In an afterword, he discusses the Holy See's contribution to the abolition movement. As a transnational actor, the Catholic Church contributes to nuclear disarmament through its teaching on the moral unacceptability of nuclear weapons and deterrence as well as through its promotion of an ethic of peace and solidarity. As a state entity, the Holy See engages the nuclear-armed states in dialogue and participates in international forums, including the Humanitarian Consequences movement and the conference that drafted the Treaty on Prohibition of Nuclear Weapons.

Notes

1. *Gaudium et spes*, no. 80.
2. *Gaudium et spes*, no. 80.
3. *Gaudium et spes*, no. 81.
4. Pope John Paul II, "Message to the United Nations General Assembly," June 7, 1982, no. 8.
5. National Conference of Catholic Bishops, *The Challenge of Peace: God's Promise and Our Response*, no. 188.
6. The treaties are the Intermediate Nuclear Forces Treaty (INF), 1987; and the Strategic Arms Reduction Talks (START), Ronald Reagan and George H. W. Bush administrations, 1991.
7. Archbishop Renato Martino, "Address to the United Nations Committee on Disarmament," November 4, 1993; citation by the US Conference of Catholic Bishops, "The Harvest of Justice Is Sown in Peace."
8. Mamberti, "Address of the Holy See to the High-Level Meeting on Disarmament," September 26, 2013.
9. See "Humanitarian Impact of Nuclear Weapons," in *Reaching Critical Will*, www.reachingcriticalwill.org/disarmament-fora/hinw.

10. Tomasi, "Statement of the Holy See at the Vienna Conference on the Humanitarian Impact of Nuclear Weapons," Vienna, December 9, 2014.
11. "Nuclear Disarmament: Time for Abolition," contributed paper of the Holy See for the Vienna Conference, December 8, 2014.
12. "Nuclear Disarmament: Time for Abolition."
13. "Nuclear Disarmament: Time for Abolition."
14. "Nuclear Disarmament: Time for Abolition."
15. "Nuclear Disarmament: Time for Abolition."
16. For the treaty, see www.un.org/disarmament/tpnw/index.html; and UN General Assembly, document A/CONF.229/2017/8.
17. For a review of events leading to a treaty and an analysis of the treaty's provisions and its potential significance, see Drew Christiansen, SJ, "The Vatican and the Ban Treaty," *Journal of Catholic Social Thought* 15, no. 1 (Winter 2018): 89–108.
18. *Gaudium et spes*, no. 80.
19. *Gaudium et spes*, no. 79.
20. See Pope Paul VI, *Octagesima adveniens* (A Call to Action), no. 50.
21. Address of His Holiness Pope Francis to Participants in the International Symposium, "Prospects for a World Free of Nuclear Weapons and for Integral Disarmament," Clementine Hall, Friday, November 10, 2017.

PART I

Setting the Agenda

1

Address by His Holiness Pope Francis

Clementine Hall, Friday, November 10, 2017

Dear Friends,

I offer a cordial welcome to each of you, and I express my deep gratitude for your presence here and your work in the service of the common good. I thank Cardinal Turkson for his greeting and introduction.

In this Symposium, you have met to discuss issues that are critical both in themselves and in the light of the complex political challenges of the current international scene, marked as it is by a climate of instability and conflict. A certain pessimism might make us think that "prospects for a world free from nuclear arms and for integral disarmament," the theme of your meeting, appear increasingly remote. Indeed, the escalation of the arms race continues unabated; and the price of modernizing and developing weaponry, not only nuclear weapons, represents a considerable expense for nations. As a result, the real priorities facing our human family, such as the fight against poverty, the promotion of peace, the undertaking of educational, ecological and healthcare projects, and the development of human rights, are relegated to second place.[1]

Nor can we fail to be genuinely concerned by the catastrophic humanitarian and environmental effects of any employment of nuclear devices. If we also take into account the risk of an accidental detonation as a result of error of any kind, the threat of their use, as well as their very possession, is to be firmly condemned. For they exist in the service of a mentality of fear that affects not only the parties in conflict but the entire human race. International relations cannot be held captive to military force, mutual intimidation, and the parading of stockpiles of arms. Weapons of mass destruction, particularly nuclear weapons, create nothing but a false sense of security. They cannot constitute the basis for peaceful coexistence between members of the human family, which must rather be inspired by an ethics of solidarity.[2] Essential in this regard is the witness given by the Hibakusha, the survivors of the bombing of Hiroshima and Nagasaki, together with other victims of nuclear arms testing. May their prophetic voice serve as a warning, above all for coming generations!

Furthermore, weapons that result in the destruction of the human race are senseless even from a tactical standpoint. For that matter, while true science is always at the service of humanity, in our time we are increasingly troubled by the misuse of certain projects originally conceived for a good cause. Suffice it to note that nuclear technologies are now spreading, also through digital communications, and that the instruments of international law have not prevented new states from joining those already in possession of nuclear weapons. The resulting scenarios are deeply disturbing if we consider the challenges of contemporary geopolitics, like terrorism or asymmetric warfare.

At the same time, a healthy realism continues to shine a light of hope on our unruly world. Recently, for example, in a historic vote at the United Nations, the majority of the members of the international community determined that nuclear weapons are not only immoral but must also be considered an illegal means of warfare. This decision filled a significant juridical lacuna, inasmuch as chemical weapons, biological weapons, antipersonnel mines and cluster bombs are all expressly prohibited by international conventions. Even more important is the fact that it was mainly the result of a "humanitarian initiative" sponsored by a significant alliance between civil society, states, international organizations, churches, academies, and groups of experts. The document that you, distinguished recipients of the Nobel Prize, have consigned to me is a part of this, and I express my gratitude and appreciation for it.

This year marks the fiftieth anniversary of the Encyclical Letter *Populorum progressio* of Pope Saint Paul VI.[3] That encyclical, in developing the Christian concept of the person, set forth the notion of integral human development and proposed it as "the new name of peace." In this memorable and still timely document, the Pope stated succinctly that "development cannot be restricted to economic growth alone. To be authentic, it must be integral; it must foster the development of each man and of the whole man" (No. 14).

We need, then, to reject the culture of waste and to care for individuals and peoples labouring under painful disparities through patient efforts to favour processes of solidarity over selfish and contingent interests. This also entails integrating the individual and the social dimensions through the application of the principle of subsidiarity, encouraging the contribution of all, as individuals and as groups. Lastly, there is a need to promote human beings in the indissoluble unity of soul and body, of contemplation and action.

In this way, progress that is both effective and inclusive can achieve the utopia of a world free of deadly instruments of aggression, contrary to the criticism of those who consider idealistic any process of dismantling arsenals. The teaching of John XXIII remains ever valid. In pointing to the goal of an integral disarmament, he stated: "Unless this process of disarmament be thoroughgoing and complete, and reach men's very souls, it is impossible to stop the arms race, or to reduce armaments, or—and this is the main thing—ultimately to abolish them entirely."[4]

The Church does not tire of offering the world this wisdom and the actions it inspires, conscious that integral development is the beneficial path that the human family is called to travel. I encourage you to carry forward this activity with patience and constancy, in the trust that the Lord is ever at our side. May he bless each of you and your efforts in the service of justice and peace. Thank you.

Notes

1. Cf. "Message to the Conference on the Humanitarian Impact of Nuclear Weapons," December 7, 2014.
2. Cf. "Message to the United Nations Conference to Negotiate a Legally Binding Instrument to Prohibit Nuclear Weapons," March 27, 2017.
3. Pope Paul VI, *Populorum progressio*, http://w2.vatican.va/content/paul-vi/en/encyclicals/documents/hf_p-vi_enc_26031967_populorum.html.
4. Pope John XXIII, *Pacem in terris*, April 11, 1963, http://w2.vatican.va/content/john-xxiii/en/encyclicals/documents/hf_j-xxiii_enc_11041963_pacem.html.

2

Address by Cardinal Pietro Parolin

In these complex and uncertain times, it may seem somewhat unrealistic, if not downright utopian, to speak of "prospects for a world free of nuclear weapons and for integral disarmament." This also seems to be confirmed by an alarming fact: the constant increase of expenditures on arms worldwide, including the costs of updating nuclear arsenals.

This meeting takes place amid this decidedly disheartening state of affairs. All the same, to speak of "prospects for a world free of nuclear weapons" invites us to reflect on a question the Holy Father asked last March 27, in his message for the opening of the United Nations Conference to Negotiate a Legally Binding Instrument to Prohibit Nuclear Weapons: Why set oneself the difficult and long-term objective of a world without nuclear arms?

It is interesting at this point to consider his carefully detailed response:

> If we take into consideration the principal threats to peace and security with their many dimensions in this multipolar world of the twenty-first century as, for example, terrorism, asymmetrical conflicts, cybersecurity, environmental problems, poverty, not a few doubts arise regarding the inadequacy of nuclear deterrence as an effective response to such challenges. These concerns are even greater when we consider the catastrophic humanitarian and environmental consequences that would follow from any use of nuclear weapons, with devastating, indiscriminate and uncontainable effects, over time and space. Similar cause for concern arises when examining the waste of resources spent on nuclear issues for military purposes, which could instead be used for worthy priorities like the promotion of peace and integral human development, as well as the fight against poverty, and the implementation of the 2030 Agenda for Sustainable Development.
>
> We need also to ask ourselves how sustainable is a stability based on fear, when it actually increases fear and undermines relationships of trust between peoples.
>
> International peace and stability cannot be based on a false sense of security, on the threat of mutual destruction or total annihilation, or on simply maintaining a balance of power.[1]

What the Holy Father has given us is a series of recommendations for a world free of nuclear weapons, which can assist in our reflections. I might summarize them under four headings:

1. The inadequacy of defense systems based on nuclear weapons in responding to threats to national and international security in the twenty-first century.
2. The catastrophic human and environmental impact of the use of nuclear weapons.
3. The waste of human and economic resources spent on updating those weapons, resources diverted from the overall pursuit of goals such as peace and integral human development.
4. The creation of a climate of fear, distrust, and conflict.

One concrete response to these issues was the recent adoption and opening for signature of the Treaty on the Prohibition of Nuclear Weapons, which was also ratified by the Holy See last September 20. The treaty encourages states not only to subscribe to it but also to attempt to understand its letter and spirit and to follow through on what it promotes. The treaty is part of the important international regime on the elimination of nuclear weapons, of which other international legal instruments are already part—for example, the Nuclear Non-Proliferation Treaty and the Nuclear Test Ban Treaty. These three instruments are complementary and are aimed at strengthening the legal norms against nuclear weapons and placing the latter in the same category as other arms of mass destruction, such as chemical and biological weapons that are already globally and universally banned by international law. The correct application of these three treaties represents a fundamental step on the road to a world free of nuclear weapons.

I would like to reflect on yet another significant aspect of this road that we are called to take. The Treaty on the Prohibition of Nuclear Weapons recognizes the importance of education for peace and for disarmament in all its aspects, together with the importance of raising awareness of the risks and consequences of nuclear weapons for current and future generations. Responding along these lines entails a commitment to significant initiatives aimed at promoting a culture that rejects nuclear weapons, a culture of life and peace, one based on the dignity of the human being and on the primacy of law. This is to be achieved by means of a multilateralism based on dialogue and the responsible, honest, and consistent cooperation of all the members of the community of nations.

At the same time, as Pope Francis pointed out in his message of last March 27, "Growing interdependence and globalization mean that any response to the threat of nuclear weapons should be collective and concerted, based on mutual trust. This trust can be built only through dialogue that is truly directed to the common good and not to the protection of veiled or particular interests; such dialogue, as far as possible, should include all."[2] Avoiding conflicts and building bridges should be the principal aim of an efficacious collective and concerted response.

It is my sincere hope that this conference will favor a reflection on the ethics of peace and multilateral security that moves beyond the fear surrounding the debate on nuclear arms and beyond the risk of an isolationism present in some current discussions. To this end, I suggest starting from one of the key ideas found in Pope Francis's encyclical *Laudato si'* on the care of our common home: from the standpoint of the "integral ecology" so clearly set forth in that text, that "everything is connected."

The idea of "integral disarmament" recalls the concept of "integral ecology." If we realize that everything is connected, it becomes all the more crucial to encourage dialogue and to create structures of trust, for these are also part of the process leading to a world free of nuclear weapons. It would be helpful if this conference could offer further points for reflection in this regard. That would involve putting into practice another key concept of *Laudato si'*, namely, the need for a change of direction on the part of the international community. In this particular case, such a change of direction should start with a reconsideration of priorities and the best ways to ensure peace and international security in the twenty-first century.

Allow me to offer one last reflection. This year marks the fiftieth anniversary of the encyclical *Populorum progressio*, which proposed

> setting aside a portion of . . . military expenditures for a world fund to relieve the needs of impoverished peoples. What is true for the immediate war against poverty is also true for the work of national development. Only a concerted effort on the part of all nations, embodied in and carried out by this world fund, will stop these senseless rivalries and promote fruitful, friendly dialogue between nations. . . . Is it not plain to everyone that such a fund would reduce the need for those other expenditures that are motivated by fear and stubborn pride? Countless millions are starving. . . . We cannot approve a debilitating arms race.[3]

This proposal of Pope Paul VI, which remains timely, might also seem unrealistic, if not utopian. Yet consideration should still be given to whether, in the process of updating the sustainable development goals adopted in 2015, it would be possible to encourage reflection on how to reintroduce it, pointing out the human and economic resources that could be saved by reduced military spending, including outlays used for the maintenance and updating of nuclear weapons. Those resources ought to be directed to the genuine goals of development and peace.

I leave this proposal to the deliberations of this assembly and of other symposiums devoted to these issues. The proposal does recognize how important it is that the international community avoid a shortsighted approach to the problems of national and global security and adopt instead *long-term action* on behalf of peace and security. As the Holy See has stated in various contexts, the pursuit of a real process of international disarmament cannot fail to produce major benefits for development. And integral human development cannot in turn fail to have profound and beneficial repercussions for issues of security.

Notes

1. "Message to the UN Conference to Negotiate a Legally Binding Instrument to Prohibit Nuclear Weapons, Leading towards their Total Elimination," New York, March 27, 2017.
2. "Message to the UN Conference."
3. Pope Saint Paul VI, encyclical letter *Populorum progressio*, March 16, 1967, nos. 51–53.

PART II

Witnesses

3

Surviving the Atomic Bomb

Masako Wada

I am very honored and deeply grateful for this opportunity to speak before you as a Hibakusha.[1] I am Wada Masako, a Hibakusha of Nagasaki. I was 22 months old when Nagasaki was devastated by the atomic bomb. My house was located 2.9 kilometers away from the blast center. Thanks to the mountains surrounding the central part of Nagasaki City, which somewhat shielded my house from the direct impact of the bomb, I have survived to this day.

On July 7, 2017, the Treaty on the Prohibition of Nuclear Weapons was adopted at the UN. After the atomic bombing of Hiroshima and Nagasaki, under the occupation of the United States, when even press reports about the atomic bombing were suppressed, Hibakusha were left abandoned without any help either from the occupying forces or from the Japanese government. It was in the wake of the nationwide people's protest against nuclear weapons, triggered by the Bikini hydrogen bomb test in 1954, that Hibakusha finally roused themselves to form Nihon Hidankyo, a national organization of Hibakusha. During the last sixty-one years since then, through our determined actions, we have called for the elimination of nuclear weapons. To the Hibakusha who have constantly appealed, "No more Hibakusha," the adoption of the Ban Treaty has given tremendous hope and courage.

We would like to share our joy with the numerous unidentified A-bomb victims who are recorded only as statistics, with the many people who have gone before us in the antinuclear movement, with our supporters in Japan and internationally, and with the members of the International Campaign to Abolish Nuclear Weapons, who received the Nobel Peace Prize for their contribution to achieving the Ban Treaty. And above all, we would like to express our deep gratitude to the Holy See for leading the debates in various international forums for the prohibition and elimination of nuclear weapons, and for becoming one of the first governments to sign and ratify the treaty.

The preamble of the treaty, which recognized the "unacceptable suffering of and harm caused to the victims of the use of nuclear weapons (Hibakusha)," clearly articulates the inhumanity of nuclear weapons. By the end of December 1945, about 210,000 people had died as a result of the bombing, including many who were killed instantly without knowing what had happened. Ninety percent of them were civilians, including elderly people and children. The deep sufferings of those who barely survived the bombing continued for a long period, even to this day—the loss of their loved ones; survivors' guilt; the scenes, sounds, and smells of the day burnt into their memories; diseases of unknown cause; economic difficulty; prejudice and discrimination in society; and many buried dreams. Those who were under the mushroom cloud—irrespective of their race, nationality, age, or sex—were forced to die or to continue to live as Hibakusha.

Because I was then only a 22-month-old baby, I do not remember anything about that time, nor can I tell you of the indescribable tragedies that our senior Hibakusha witnessed and experienced on that day and in the aftermath. But I was certainly there, together with my mother and grandfather. Allow me to share with you a little about what my mother used to tell me over and over again.

On August 9, after an air-raid warning was lifted, my mother was preparing lunch. I was playing alone on the floor of the entrance. At 11:02, she heard a big sound of an explosion. The next moment, windowpanes, sliding doors, and clay walls inside our house were all blown to pieces by the blast. A pile of mud and dust over 30 centimeters thick was left on the floor. Outside, my mother saw orange-colored smoke, which veiled the houses on the other side of the street. The green trees on the mountainsides surrounding the downtown area had turned brown.

On the mountain roads, she saw a file of people escaping from fires like ants, moving down over the mountain toward our area. They all looked brown with their scantily clad bodies burned all over and with their hair matted with blood and standing on end like horns.

The empty lot next to our house became a cremation ground, where dead bodies collected by garbage carts were brought in and incinerated day after day. My mother said that everyone soon became numb to the growing number of corpses and even to the stench from burning bodies. What is human dignity? Humans are not created to be treated like this.

She went to help medical staff at a temporary aid station, but she fainted at the sight of victims with horrible burns and injuries laid all over the floor. The next task allocated to her was to use a broom to remove maggots swarming on the wounds of the victims. They were so numerous and as big as your thumb.

The US military dropped a radio sensor with a parachute from the B-29, along with the atomic bomb. It was an instrument to measure the destructive power of the atomic bomb, including the blast pressure, intensity, and heat generated by the explosion. My mother used to say she wondered why that device did not provide the US military with information about the lives of the people and their families under the mushroom cloud, and the preciousness of human life.

My mother died six years ago at the age of eighty-nine. She was in and out of the hospital twenty-eight times due to numerous illnesses, including heart troubles, stomach cancer, and liver cancer. Before she died, I once recorded what she witnessed in writing, but she seemed quite dissatisfied with what she read. She might have felt that no words or expressions could describe the hellish scenes she had witnessed.

Other senior Hibakusha must feel the same as she did. I always feel hesitant to share my mother's experience with other people, as I know I can never fully describe what really happened. But now that seventy-two years have passed, the average age of the survivors has reached eighty-one, and we younger Hibakusha must succeed their work and speak out on their behalf.

Nuclear weapons are inhuman weapons that will bring indiscriminate and widespread damage to the victims from the blast, from the heat rays and radiation, and from aftereffects that last for many years. If they are ever used again, the same suffering that the Hibakusha have gone through will be inflicted on many people all over the world. In Nihon Hidankyo's founding statement "Message to the World" of 1956, we declared: "Our will to save humanity from its crisis through the lessons learned from our experiences, while at the same time saving ourselves." With this pledge, we have continued to work for the elimination of nuclear weapons. With the adoption of the treaty, a heavy and rusty door has begun to open, and we are finally seeing a ray of light illuminating a path to achieve our goal.

Hibakusha have given testimonies on their experiences across the world, despite the painful memories drawing them back to those two days. We note the word "public conscience" stated in the preamble of the treaty. "Public conscience" is essential for securing the benefit for the public, the human race, and Mother Earth. Power is not justice. Nuclear weapons are an injustice that must be abolished by the responsibility of the humans who made them. It is the role of public conscience and justice to pray and to accumulate small efforts for achieving the elimination of nuclear weapons. We must continue to urge the nuclear-armed states and their allies, including Japan, to sign and ratify the Treaty on the Prohibition of Nuclear Weapons.

In April 2016 we started the International Signature Campaign in Support of the Appeal of the Hibakusha for the Elimination of Nuclear Weapons. To date, we have submitted more than 5.15 million signatures to the United Nations. We set our goal to achieve hundreds of millions of signatures by 2020 all over the world, by rallying the public conscience of many people. I sincerely ask each one of you here today, as representatives of civil society, as human beings with dignity and as peacemakers, to raise a loud voice from the Vatican for achieving the abolition of nuclear weapons.

Note

1. "Hibakusha" refers to a survivor of either of the atomic bomb attacks on Hiroshima and Nagasaki in 1945; from *Collins English Dictionary*, 12th ed. (Glasgow: HarperCollins, 2014). —Editors.

4

Hiroshima's Heritage and the Role of Companies in City Reconstruction: How This Experience Shaped Today's Values

Bruno L. Müller

I am aware that many of the participants in this conference have visited Hiroshima, which is Mazda's hometown. I want to briefly explore the link between Hiroshima and Mazda, the company's role in rebuilding a city destroyed by the atomic bomb, and how it has influenced and reinforced our values to this day.

Allow me to start with a personal memory: Back in 1991, I had the opportunity for the first time in my life to spend a longer period at Mazda's world headquarters in Hiroshima. Visiting the Hiroshima Peace Memorial Museum for the first time, I was moved to tears by the sheer brutality of the morning of August 6, 1945, when the atomic bomb exploded over the city. I felt despair and deep sadness.

During my stay in Hiroshima, however, I also observed something that is unique to the people of the city: they always look ahead, making a priority of promoting peace to ensure that such a catastrophic event never happens again. For me personally, seeing something positive come out of such a tragedy was very comforting.

Mazda has been in Hiroshima for almost a hundred years and is an integral part of the city. In 1920 Jujiro Matsuda founded the company, which launched its first vehicle, a three-wheeled truck called the Mazda-Go, in 1931.

Obviously, that day in August 1945 changed the lives of the 340,000 people who were in Hiroshima, including those at Mazda. The blast at 8:16 a.m. caused unimaginable devastation, killing about 80,000 instantly. The death toll would rise to 140,000 by the end of the year. Mazda was somewhat spared; its factory and headquarters were shielded by a mountain, so they survived mostly unscathed. Part of the headquarters would even house the Hiroshima prefectural government, whose buildings were destroyed. However, employees lost family and friends; countless loved ones perished.

The Matsuda family felt obligated to help rebuild the city as quickly as possible, and Mazda was able to resume vehicle production after only four months. The affordable Mazda-Go trucks helped survivors cope with their day-to-day needs while also facilitating reconstruction efforts. They became a symbol of courage and hope for the people of Hiroshima. These experiences had a major impact on Mazda, further shaping our values and ethical principles.

Today, Mazda is active in more than 130 countries. In this globalized world, Mazda's people and partners come from many different countries, speak different languages, and have different cultural backgrounds. However, the challenger spirit—an attitude of never giving up, also known as the Mukainada spirit, which is named after Mazda's home district in Hiroshima—runs deeply in everyone at Mazda. Today, as much as ever, it connects each of us with Hiroshima's heritage and helps us work together across borders to succeed and enrich the lives of our customers.

Indeed, this heritage and these entrenched values inspire the people at Mazda to continually challenge convention and make things better—for people, for the planet, and for society. Our corporate culture promotes a hierarchy in which universal human values drive business objectives. Our human-centered development philosophy clearly illustrates this. At Mazda, we design vehicles around the driver and passengers, putting the people first.

But this philosophy applies beyond cars to everything we do, from constantly striving to improve the ecological footprint at all levels of the organization to treating colleagues, partners, and customers with respect. It is also reflected in Mazda's commitment to organizations that make a difference, such as the SOS Children's Villages and the World Summit of Nobel Peace Laureates. Because Hiroshima's history—our history—serves as a constant reminder that we need to put aside our differences and work together.

In the words of Gandhi, an ounce of practice is worth tons of preaching.[1] Breaking down hate and building up mutual respect are not easy. They take patience. Particularly today, peace cannot be taken for granted. But we must persevere. It is our duty.

As Pope Francis said, "Indifference is dangerous, whether innocent or not."[2] And we hope that this testimony about Hiroshima's spirit of never giving up, a spirit Mazda wholeheartedly shares, will inspire all of us to continue promoting peace every day.

Notes

1. According to the Gandhi Peace Foundation in New Delhi, he said this many times in various forms, referring to an old proverb. *Gandhi Marg: A Quarterly Journal of Gandhian Thought* 9–10, 1965.
2. Homily, May 25, 2003.

PART III

Laureates

5

Letter from Nobel Peace Prize Laureates to His Holiness Pope Francis on the Occasion of the International Conference

*Mohamed ElBaradei, Mairead Corrigan-Maguire,
Adolfo Pérez Esquivel, Jody Williams,
and Muhammad Yunus*

Your Holiness,

We welcome with deep gratitude the attention that you give to the pressing issues of our time. In particular, at this moment of deep tension among nuclear-armed states, we applaud your new initiatives to achieve world peace and to tackle nuclear weapons as well as integral disarmament overall.

The successful conclusion of negotiations at the United Nations on July 7, 2017, for a comprehensive international treaty prohibiting nuclear weapons, despite the lack of participation of the nuclear-armed states, creates a way toward a world free of nuclear weapons. This convention will begin to establish a new international legal regulation and further stigmatize those weapons and the states that so far refuse to give them up. It is worth remembering that even those states that did not support the 2017 Treaty on the Prohibition of Nuclear Weapons but are parties to the Nuclear Non-Proliferation Treaty are still under the obligation set out in its Article VI: "Each of the Parties to the Treaty undertakes to pursue negotiations in good faith on effective measures relating to cessation of the nuclear arms race at an early date and to nuclear disarmament, and on a Treaty on general and complete disarmament under strict and effective international control."

It was the concerted action of civil society, religious communities, international organizations, and the states that fervently desire a nuclear-free world that resulted in the successful nuclear ban treaty negotiations at the United Nations. Ultimately, it will be the ongoing work of these sectors of society that will open the way for nuclear states to finally relinquish these weapons that are capable of obliterating life as we know it in the blink of an eye. It will not be an easy task, but it is possible.

The only way to assure a world-sustainable peace and to prevent nuclear weapons from spreading and ultimately being used is to abolish them. At the same time, we must build an inclusive and equitable international security system in which no country feels the need to rely on nuclear weapons. Eliminating nuclear weapons alone would release resources to make this shift. With integral disarmament, the possibilities are limitless.

We need to create a mechanism for multinational control of the production of fissile material. This would counteract an emerging phenomenon of more and more countries becoming nuclear-weapon-capable states, possessing the technology that could be used to make nuclear weapons, if they so choose. For any such mechanism to succeed, however, it must be universal, equitable, and apolitical.

As we focus on complete nuclear disarmament, we must also keep our attention on emerging lethal autonomous weapons systems that on their own could target and kill human beings. It is imperative to ask ourselves how ethical and moral human beings can possibly believe that it is fine to give machines the ability to kill humans. The best solution to this impending third revolution in warfare is to preemptively ban such weapons before they appear on the battlefield.

Banning nuclear weapons and promoting peace and an integral disarmament means putting humanity first and putting our minds together to meet the serious challenges we face—to name just a few: climate change; a globalized economy that glorifies the accumulation of wealth for wealth's sake and cares little for meeting the needs of the majority of the billions of people sharing our planet; and terrorism of all kinds, including that of the state.

National security frameworks that rely on weapons, militaries, and the projection of state power cannot possibility protect us from the challenges of today's world. It is time to recognize that real security comes from placing the focus on meeting the needs of individuals and communities—human security—and protecting and promoting the common good.

Your Holiness, thank you for your efforts to benefit all humanity. We are ready to support your new disarmament initiatives in any way that would prove useful.

Mohamed ElBaradei
Mairead Corrigan-Maguire
Adolfo Pérez Esquivel
Jody Williams
Muhammad Yunus

6

Nuclear Weapons: Confronting Armageddon

Mohamed ElBaradei

It is an honor to take part in this conference, a laudable initiative by the Vatican. Nuclear weapons are the most urgent threat facing humanity today, and the risk of their use is higher than any time in the recent past. There is a growing mind-set of *Carthago delenda est* (Carthage must be destroyed). It reveals itself in senseless and dehumanizing conflicts; in horrific terrorism; in intangible walls between cultures and people; in an atmosphere of fear and exclusion and of chest-beating by nuclear weapon states. The urgent question on many people's minds is naturally how we can avert war and self-annihilation. I will first paint a broad picture of our world as I see it, as a necessary backdrop for discussing the current status of nuclear weapons.

Our quest for peace has always been elusive. Wars have dominated the human timeline since recorded history. Hundreds of millions have lost their lives to violence perpetuated under the guise of religion, nationalism, ethnicity, and other alleged *casus belli*.[1] We organized ourselves in social units of city-states, empires, and sovereign states. We had the Peace of Westphalia, the Congress of Vienna, the League of Nations, and the United Nations to regulate international relations. We created security systems based on a balance of power and later on collective security. But peace has remained fleeting and fragile, with force and violence continuing to be our primary choices to settle differences.

Our human condition of late has become more absurd and contradictory: we have made a huge leap forward in the way we understand our world and ourselves. But at the same time we have failed dismally to translate these advances into values and actions to uphold human dignity. We are simultaneously showing every day without shame not only how high we can soar but also how low we can sink.

War, poverty, and tyranny, and their assault on human dignity—aptly described by the American statesman Adlai Stevenson in the 1950s as the "great enemies of man"—remain as shocking today. In the recent past, the international community did little more than wring its hands while literally millions of innocent civilians were slaughtered in Rwanda, Congo, Darfur, Afghanistan, Syria, and other places. We continue to judge the sanctity of life according to who is dying and where. And the response to humanitarian disasters is mostly informed by geostrategic interests.

Poverty and hunger, although they have decreased in the last two decades, continue at miserable levels. According to the World Bank, 767 million people live in extreme poverty on less than $1.90 a day, and 2.1 billion people live on less than $3.10 a day, the median poverty line. Millions die every year because of a lack of access to medical care. And inequality in the distribution of wealth between and within countries has reached obscene levels.

Brutal repression continues to be the hallmark of a third of the world's nations. Uprisings against tyranny and injustice and in the quest for human dignity continue, mostly in the Arab world and Africa. But the trampling of human rights by authoritarian regimes is becoming almost a spectator sport for the international community, limited mostly to cynical expressions of "deep concern." All the options used to counter tyranny—regime change, dumb sanctions, or "embracing" the despots and arming them to the teeth—have only added to rising extremism and decaying values.

Poverty, inequality, and repression are the most lethal weapons of mass destruction. The plight of the poor, deprived of the most basic needs; the predicament of millions of young people with dashed hopes; the despair of the tortured and oppressed—all create a poisonous environment of anger and humiliation, and a fertile breeding ground for extremism and nihilism.

Violence and radicalism continue to manifest themselves wearing different masks of ideology, religion, ethnicity, or nationalism to justify the most heinous acts. And in many cases conflicts are hijacked by outside powers looking for geopolitical gains in proxy wars. But in the end, innocent civilians foot the bill, and they are callously described as "collateral damage."

In 2016 the number of refugees forced to flee their homes as a result of violence and war reached an estimated 65 million people, over 21 million of whom were forced to flee their country altogether. The global response to the refugee crisis continues to be wretched. Obviously the solution to the refugee crisis is not through a population transfer. But we need to address the roots of the problem: persecution, repression, poverty, extremism, and war. And even at the level of humanitarian assistance, international humanitarian organizations continue to almost beg to secure the minimum resources to provide the absolute basic needs. This travesty is not because we are short of money; it is a result of our skewed priorities. We only devote about 1 percent of the $1.7 trillion we spend on armaments per year to disaster relief and peacekeeping operations combined.

In our interlocked world, our most ominous threats have no borders: terrorism, climate change, weapons of mass destruction, communicable diseases, cybercrime, illegal immigration, and illicit drugs. Our actions or nonactions eventually come back to haunt us wherever we are. No part of the world can remain quarantined any longer.

We are facing an outright crisis of governance: governments that pursue short-term myopic policies, both informed and hamstrung by party politics, that fail to cope with people's expectations or meet new long-term global challenges. As a result, populism is on the rise and social cohesion is fraying. There is a pull and push in conflicting directions—movements to integrate into larger social units, but also movements to split into smaller ones. The tension between the national and the global is distinctly palpable.

At the international level, institutions suffer from structural deficiencies and a lack of authority and resources. They are steadily becoming polarized and paralyzed. The chronic failure of the UN Security Council to take the necessary preventive measures or provide consistent and adequate responses to threats to international peace and security is a stark case in point, a symbol of a dysfunctional system of collective security.

Against this background, the reliance on nuclear weapons as the centerpiece of our collective security system is horrifying. The argument that nuclear weapons have kept the peace is bogus and does not withstand scrutiny. A peace that hangs on a doctrine of "mutually assured destruction" is based on the anachronistic premise that "some are more equal than others"; is underpinned by human fallibility; and, in addition, is irrelevant to extremists. It is a peace that is unsustainable and highly perilous. The reality is that we continue to live under Damocles' sword and are sleepwalking into an apocalypse.

The truth is that the very existence of nuclear weapons bears the seeds of their proliferation because they continue to be seen as the ultimate security deterrence and a major source of global influence. That some countries possess them—or are protected by them within an alliance, while others are asked not to have them—is oxymoronic in the long term. As I mentioned earlier, you cannot credibly ask a person not to smoke while you are dangling a cigarette from your mouth. With the technology out of the box, we should not be surprised if other countries, particularly in areas of conflict, will seek to acquire them to mimic the "big boys." Some have the capability to churn up nuclear weapons in a matter of months. Recent history should be our guide. But more ominously, how long will it take before a terrorist group with no return address lays its hands on a nuclear weapon or a dirty bomb?

Almost all prominent statesmen have argued forcefully that reliance on nuclear weapons is becoming "increasingly hazardous and decreasingly effective." In 2011 former US secretary of defense Bill Perry talked about three false alarms he knew of, in which Soviet missiles were thought to be screaming toward the United States. He added: "To this day I believe that we avoided nuclear catastrophe as much by good luck as by good management." In 2008, Senator Sam Nunn, a leading US defense expert, stated, "I believe that America would be far more secure if no one had nuclear weapons." Former US defense secretary Robert McNamara, a one-time staunch supporter of nuclear weapons, put it in blunter terms: "The indefinite combination of human fallibility and nuclear weapons will lead to the destruction of nations." This led him to the conclusion that "the only way to eliminate the risk is to eliminate nuclear weapons."

But with all these warnings and many others from different parts of the world, have we seriously started to take meaningful steps to get rid of nuclear weapons? Have we seriously tried to drastically reduce the number of weapons in existence? Have we seriously tried to alter the nuclear launch warning system, the so-called prompt launch, where a US or a Russian president has a mere 7 to 8 minutes to respond to a "reported" nuclear attack, with the odds of miscalculation increasing exponentially as a result of cyber manipulation? Have we seriously tried to reduce our reliance on nuclear weapons in national security strategies? And have we seriously started thinking about the security architecture in a nuclear-weapon-free world?

It borders on insanity that, more than a quarter of a century after the end of the Cold War, we still have almost 15,000 nuclear weapons, about 2,000 of which are still on high alert. Churchill chuckled way back when that "if you go on with this nuclear arms race, all you are going to do is make the rubble bounce."

Under the Nuclear Non-Proliferation Treaty (NPT), the so-called five weapon-states parties not only have an obligation to negotiate in good faith toward nuclear disarmament but equally, in the words of the International Court of Justice, have "the obligation to achieve a precise result: nuclear disarmament in all its aspects."

However, after almost five decades, the nuclear weapon states are moving in the completely opposite direction. They are modernizing their arsenals to the tune of hundreds of billions of dollars. Some of them cannot even commit to a ban on nuclear testing. As a result, the Comprehensive Nuclear Test Ban Treaty, which was concluded in 1996, has yet to enter into force. And for the last twenty years, the proposal to conclude the Fissile Material Cut-Off Treaty to prohibit the further production of fissile material for nuclear weapons has been dead in its tracks.

In 2003, as director-general of the International Atomic Energy Agency (IAEA), I called for a new approach to curb the proliferation of the sensitive parts of the fuel cycle, uranium enrichment and plutonium separation, by bringing it under international control. The recently inaugurated LEU Bank in Kazakhstan, owned and operated by the IAEA, is a step in the right direction. But true security regarding the fuel cycle can only come through the multilateralization of all uranium enrichment and plutonium separation facilities. This is regrettably yet again not being seriously discussed and thus is not in the cards in the foreseeable future.

What is more distressing, in addition, is that recent reports indicate that the United States has increased the targeting and killing capability of its ballistic missile force, and therefore its capacity for a surprise attack to fight and win a nuclear war. Experts tell us that this will only lead to the deepening of mistrust, the hardening of an already aggressive nuclear posture, and the increased possibility of a nuclear response to a false alarm. This entire landscape is frightening and shameful. It shows no genuine commitment whatsoever to nuclear disarmament. And it undermines the legal and moral foundation of the nonproliferation effort.

The recently concluded Treaty on the Prohibition of Nuclear Weapons, adopted by 122 states (69 states did not vote), which prohibits the acquisition of nuclear weapons and asks the weapon states to shed their nuclear weapons, grew out of a rising awareness of the catastrophic humanitarian consequences of any use of nuclear weapons, along with their constant threat to humanity and all life on Earth.

It was equally the result of the frustration at the snail's pace of nuclear disarmament. Its adoption was a logical step. The international community has already prohibited biological and chemical weapons, land mines, and cluster munitions, classes of weapons that are less destructive than nuclear weapons. Nuclear weapons were therefore, until the conclusion of the new convention, a historical oddity.

Deplorably, none of the nuclear weapon states adopted this convention. Instead, the United States, the United Kingdom, and France quickly declared that they "do not intend to ever become party," because the convention "is incompatible with the policy of nuclear deterrence, which has been essential to keeping the peace in Europe and North Asia for over 70 years." But is not this precisely the policy of nuclear deterrence that the NPT aimed to abolish when it obligated the weapon states to negotiate in good faith toward nuclear disarmament? And was not that obligation an essential part of the "bargain," so to speak, under which all other states agreed not to acquire nuclear weapons?

Other NATO members and close allies of the weapon states also rejected the idea of the convention and did not participate in its adoption. They argued that it would be ineffective in eliminating nuclear weapons and could adversely affect regional and global security. But there are a few questions here: Is the obligation in good faith to achieve nuclear disarmament, agreed upon almost fifty years ago, an open-ended one with no time limit? Does not the prohibition of nuclear weapons as a step toward their elimination strengthen the overarching goal of the NPT? And was not that the path followed to eliminate other weapons of mass destruction—prohibit and eliminate? And finally, how about the security of those who do not have nuclear weapons or benefit from their protection? Does their security or insecurity count?

To my mind, the reaction of the nuclear weapon states and their allies is a lopsided, if not condescending, view of "collective" security. One would have expected the weapon states and those in their camps to at least, in the words of the Norwegian Nobel Committee, "initiate serious negotiations with a view to the gradual, balanced, and carefully monitored elimination" of nuclear weapons, rather than this negative reaction. I still very much hope that the views of the weapon states will evolve in this direction over time. A sharp global division over the very core of collective security is dangerous to all.

Every state, irrespective of the nature or orientation of its security regime, will do all it can to protect itself against perceived threats and insecurity. We must therefore urgently work for an equitable, inclusive, and reliable system of security. In such a system, weapons of mass destruction cannot have a place.

War, poverty, and tyranny—our perpetual enemies—are of our own making. They are the outcome of an environment we have constructed and a mind-set we have cultivated. They all lead to the loss of human dignity, which in turn continues to fuel them. This vicious circle must be broken. We need a new global paradigm where we genuinely subscribe to the values we often reference but rarely pursue: the sanctity of life, equity, inclusiveness and diversity, solidarity, and dialogue, rather than double standards, polarization, humiliation, exclusion, and the use of force.

The challenges we all face are bigger than any single country, conflict, or issue, and none of us can or will prevail alone. We will either swim together or sink together. Somehow, we have lost our way. It is time to adjust our mind-set to save ourselves from ourselves.

Note

1. Defined as "an act of justifying, or regarded as a reason for, war" by the *Oxford English Dictionary*. —Editors.

7

For the Disarmament of Injustice

Adolfo Pérez Esquivel

We are confronting great challenges in the twenty-first century. The end of the Cold War seemed as though it might offer the possibility of a significant reduction in defense spending, which could eventually create the conditions for a more equitable international order between the developed and capitalist countries of the North and the underdeveloped and dependent countries of the South.

An idealized and naive vision of globalization predicted that the integration of regional blocs would result in the deactivation of old threats and potential conflicts, a fact that incentivized the reduction of defense spending and, in particular, spending designated for the production of arms.

The new international order, or rather the order of institutionalized injustice, has instead generated a context of greater uncertainty and diminished capacity for regulating potentially explosive national and regional conflicts, which, in many cases, had their origins in military interventions led by the great powers.

The military interventions against Iraq permit an assessment of the interventions of the great powers in the destruction of a country. I was in Iraq after Operation Desert Storm, and I saw images of civilians in antiaircraft shelters that were annihilated by missiles and whose shadows remained seared upon the walls.

These bombardments were perpetrated in the name of "democracy," just as in the former Yugoslavia and in Afghanistan, where depleted uranium was incorporated in the construction of pumps. Depleted uranium has a prolonged residual impact over time and generates a serious impact on health, as well as irreversible ecological damage. The prohibition of weapons with depleted uranium is still an ongoing issue.

Certainly, the dictatorial regimes that existed before these interventions were under investigation for violations of human rights, but this situation does not justify military invasions, and even less so the use of such theaters of war for the development of weapons with ever more destructive force.

This English translation by Julia Young, an associate professor in the Department of History at the Catholic University of America, is followed by the original Spanish. —Editors.

Defense spending has increased, and growing fiscal deficits and financial crises have not significantly affected this trajectory. This is not a coincidence; the earnings obtained from the financial and production systems are derived in large measure from the military-technological system, the war industry, and the arms race, and do not fund development or the redistribution of income. Nuclear weapons reinforce this logic, and today we face an outlook that is every day more worrisome. Pope Francis said it well in his encyclical *Laudato si'*, referring to the knowledge and the strength acquired by technologies such as nuclear power, which grant "an impressive dominance over the whole of humanity and the entire world. Never has humanity had such power over itself, yet nothing ensures that it will be used wisely, particularly when we consider how it is currently being used."

The false promises of integration and economic cooperation that fueled the process of globalization were revealed to be nothing more than the defense of multinational companies' profits. Freedom of trade and economic opening were accompanied by military expansion and the exponential growth of spending on the arms race, all at the expense of human welfare.

How can we confront this situation? In the arena of international protest and mobilization, it is necessary to strongly emphasize the reduction of both military spending and the production of weapons.

Today, multilateral regulatory organizations either do not exist, in the case of finances, or are too weak or insufficient, in the case of security systems, to resolve conflicts. In order to prevent and resolve new and old conflicts, we must advance the disarmament of injustice. To attain this objective, we should construct social coalitions capable of making an impact at the institutional level, in order to involve states in the construction of a new international order that is democratic, egalitarian, and just.

For multilateral organizations, the challenge lies in increasing their capacity to regulate and resolve conflicts. International arms control treaties, such as the Nuclear Non-Proliferation Treaty, exemplify cases in which the construction of international legitimacy has resulted in better control, prohibition of weapons, progressive disarmament, and the peaceful use of nuclear energy.

Numerous countries usually adhere to treaties that establish a common path, although at certain moments such treaties tend to become less effective, and to generate a lower capacity to regulate and resolve problems. In these cases, the challenge is to reinforce multilateral and regional initiatives that allow for modifications to perceptions of threat and promote strategies for building mutual trust, which foster the development of more comprehensive solutions. Accordingly, regional initiatives have achieved meaningful contributions, such as the Treaty for the Prohibition of Nuclear Arms in Latin America and the Caribbean—known as the Treaty of Tlatelolco—which established the denuclearization of the territory of Latin America and the Caribbean.

Initiatives for the declaration of "nuclear-free zones of peace" are an integral part of a global peacebuilding strategy. Such initiatives seek to promote mutual trust and collective security, in order to avoid an escalation of the presence of the great powers in zones that are subject to hegemonic dispute.

I would like to point out various initiatives in which we participated, such as the South American Commission for Peace, Regional Security, and Democracy, created in April 1987, which proposed early on to create a Zone of Peace in South America.

Latin American governments promoted the creation of the Union of South American Nations, which has moved toward common defense policies, as well as the Community of Latin American and Caribbean States (CELAC). These organizations now represent a way for "Our America" to solve conflicts and foster common development policies. Thus, in 2014 Latin America and the Caribbean was declared a "Zone of Peace" in the historic Havana Declaration of CELAC, despite the fact that it had been impossible to accomplish this designation for all the Americas within the framework of the Organization of American States at the Conference of Defense Ministers of the Americas in 2012, because both the United States and Canada opposed the initiative.

And this opposition is no accident: the United Kingdom has consolidated a military base in the Falkland Islands in the South Atlantic, which represents an unjustified and disproportionate presence outside NATO and threatens regional security. This threat is reinforced by the presence of nuclear submarines with the capacity to carry nuclear arms, which violates international treaties that have established that this zone should be denuclearized.

In brief, international and regional treaties that advance the objectives of arms prohibition, disarmament, and zones of peace are agreements that create a framework of institutions and rules that—notwithstanding the fact that in some cases these treaties have weaknesses and limitations in their ability to resolve conflicts—pave the way for the peaceful resolution of conflicts by strategic actors with the capacity to advocate and veto, which agree to participate in cooperative solutions and disarmament.

Confronted with this situation, the people play an indispensable role in bolstering compliance with these treaties, as well as expanding and incorporating other complementary and convergent initiatives in favor of peace, development with social justice, and democracy.

We have various experiences along this path: the encyclical *Pacem in terris*, by Pope John XXIII, stated that people are living in fear due to continuous warfare, armed conflict in various regions of the world, and an increase of nuclear weapons that puts the life of people and the planetary system at risk. This encyclical also calls on the conscience of the people to urgently demand "a cessation to the arms race. The stockpiles of armaments which have been built up in various countries must be reduced all round and simultaneously by the parties concerned. Nuclear weapons must be banned." Pope John XXIII pointed this out in 1963; we should ask ourselves what humanity has done in the intervening years, and where humanity is in the present.[1]

The World Social Forum has been a beacon for confronting neoliberal politics, free trade agreements, the activities of the international financial system and the major multinational corporations, and the arms race—all of which are responsible for the subjugation and exploitation of our peoples. From there originated the hope that "Another World Is Possible" for the development of numerous popular movements.

Faced with the challenge of climate change, there are instances of coordination, such as those convened by the Plurinational State of Bolivia, where social movements from all over the world clearly explained that climate change is the result of a system of plunder and depredation that today threatens the survival of the planet. This platform has offered renewed hope for "Good Living," that is, alternative development strategies tailored to our realities.

We can also highlight the proposals by global labor unions for the Democratization of Energy, which are being advanced in a time of ever-growing emergencies, in recognition that access to energy is a human right. At the same time, alternative sources of clean and renewable energy are being developed as part of the search for alternate modes of production and development.

The International Campaign to Abolish Nuclear Weapons, which was awarded the Nobel Peace Prize in 2017, is an excellent example of an initiative born in civil society, which joins with governments willing to lead in devising a treaty banning nuclear weapons. Although the principal countries that possess nuclear weapons oppose the ban, the treaty points the way forward and contributes to pressure that can advance multilateral agreements on the reduction and suppression of these weapons of mass destruction.

We the people have our moments of dialogue and coordination, and although we sometimes have our differences, given the plurality of expressions that manifest themselves in the civil societies of each country, in general we are in agreement.

The principal challenge is finding ways to enhance cooperation and initiatives for disarmament when the dominant powers do nothing but provoke, wound, and plunder the peoples of the world. In particular the main power, the United States, which has placed itself in the leading role of multilateralism, appears now to have embarked a strategy of permanent provocation and, as we would say in Spanish, "upending the gameboard" of the multilateral organizations in order to redesign them even more in its own image and likeness.

Recently we witnessed an escalation of threats between North Korea and the United States. The worrying development of nuclear weapons and long-range missiles on the part of North Korea, as well as the growing interventions of the United States in military maneuvers in the Asian region, have led the current president of the United States to threaten the total destruction of North Korea. The fact that the greatest power on the planet is threatening another country with extermination represents a situation of unusual gravity that alters and imperils the very principles of coexistence formulated by the United Nations.

To confront this problem, several Nobel laureates have called for a peaceful dialogue between the United States and North Korea, requesting that the secretary-general of the United Nations deploy a proactive negotiation strategy in order to work on nonaggression agreements that would place a moratorium on nuclear testing and halt military exercises, among other measures that would foster the construction of peace agreements and avoid the escalation of threats and aggressions.

The multilateral system presents impediments to the settlement of conflicts, no matter the challenge at hand. The struggles for the protection of individual rights and human rights, the defense of the environment, the processes of disarmament, and the achievement of justice all require strengthening the self-determination of the people, in all corners of the world. The results are not assured. But if we do not try, we risk being complicit in a globalized order that, in ever-new guises, insists on maintaining a disorder of institutionalized injustice. The challenge for the future of humanity lies in the decision of the people to stop being spectators and to assume their role as creators of their own lives and their own stories.

Por el desarme de la injusticia

Estamos frente a grandes desafíos en el siglo XXI. El fin de la guerra fría parecía ofrecer la posibilidad de una significativa reducción de los gastos de defensa, que podían eventualmente ser usados para la reestructuración de un orden internacional más equitativo entre los países del Norte, capitalista desarrollado y los países del Sur subdesarrollo y dependiente.

Una visión idílica e ingenua del proceso de globalización auguraba que los procesos de integración de bloques regionales tendían a desactivar viejas amenazas e hipótesis de conflictos, hecho que favorecía la reducción de los gastos en defensa y en particular de los destinados a la producción de armamentos.

El nuevo orden internacional, o mejor dicho el orden de injusticias institucionalizado, ha generado un contexto de mayor incertidumbre y de menor capacidad de regular conflictos nacionales y regionales que pueden detonar y en muchos casos derivaron en intervenciones militares lideradas por las grandes potencias.

Las intervenciones militares contra Irak permiten evaluar las injerencias de las grandes potencias en la destrucción de un país. He estado en Irak después de la operación Tormenta del Desierto y he visto en refugios antiaéreos las imágenes de población civil que fueron desintegradas por misiles y sus sombras quedaron impresas en las paredes.

Fueron bombardeos perpetrados en nombre de la "democracia," al igual que en la ex Yugoslavia y en Afganistán, donde incorporaron en la construcción de las bombas, uranio empobrecido que tiene un impacto residual prolongado en el tiempo y generan un alto impacto en la salud y un daño ecológico irreversible. La prohibición de armas con uranio empobrecido es todavía un tema pendiente.

Ciertamente que los regímenes dictatoriales preexistentes a dichas intervenciones eran objeto de fuertes cuestionamientos por violaciones a los derechos humanos, pero dicha situación no justifica las invasiones militares y menos el uso de esos escenarios bélicos para el desarrollo de armamentos con poder cada vez más destructivos.

Los gastos en defensa se han incrementado, y los crecientes déficits fiscales y las crisis financieras no han tenido mayor impacto en afectar esa progresión. Esto no es casual, las ganancias obtenidas del sistema financiero y productivo se derivan en gran medida al sistema tecnológico militar, la industria bélica y la carrera armamentista, no va al desarrollo y la distribución de ingresos. El armamento nuclear refuerza esta lógica y hoy tenemos un panorama cada día más preocupante. Bien lo expresó el Papa Francisco en su Encíclica Laudato Sí, al referirse al conocimiento y el poder que adquieren ciertas tecnologías, como la nuclear, que otorgan "un dominio impresionante sobre el conjunto de la humanidad y del mundo entero. Nunca la humanidad tuvo tanto poder sobre sí misma y nada garantiza que vaya a utilizarlo bien, sobre todo si se considera el modo como lo está haciendo."

Las expectativas de integración y cooperación económica que impulsarían los procesos de globalización terminaron evidenciando su verdadera faz en la defensa de la tasa de ganancia de las transnacionales. La libertad de comercio, la apertura económica, vinieron así aseguradas por el expansionismo militar, y al crecimiento geométrico del gasto en la carrera armamentista, en desmedro del bienestar de los pueblos.

¿Qué podemos hacer frente a esto?

En el terreno de la denuncia y movilización internacional, urge fortalecer en las luchas actuales una perspectiva de reducción de la producción de armamentos y de los gastos militares.

Hoy los organismos multilaterales de regulación, o no existen, como en el caso de las finanzas, o son débiles o insuficientes, como en los sistemas de seguridad, como para resolver conflictos. El desafío para prevenir y resolver las causas de viejos y nuevos conflictos, es avanzar en el desarme de la injusticia. Para alcanzar ese objetivo, debemos construir coaliciones sociales con capacidad de incidencia institucional, para involucrar a los estados en construir un nuevo orden institucional internacional democrático, igualitario y justo.

El desafío de los organismos multilaterales es poder incrementar su capacidad de regular y resolver conflictos. Los tratados internacionales de control de armamentos, como el Tratado de No Proliferación Nuclear, constituyen instancias de construcción de legitimidad internacional en favor de un mayor control, prohibición de armamentos, de progresivo desarme y uso pacífico de la energía nuclear.

Numerosos países suelen adherir a estos tratados que fijan un derrotero común a seguir, aunque en cierto momento presentan una suerte de a-mesetamiento y menor capacidad de regulación y resolución de problemas. En estos casos se presenta el desafío de reforzar iniciativas multilaterales y regionales que permitan modificar las percepciones de amenaza y favorecer estrategias de construcción de confianza mutua, que permitan avanzar en soluciones más de fondo. En este sentido, las iniciativas regionales han realizado aportes significativos, como es el Tratado para la Prohibición de Armas Nucleares en América Latina y el Caribe -conocido como Tratado de Tlatelolco- que establece la desnuclearización del territorio de América Latina y el Caribe.

Las iniciativas por la declaración de "zonas de paz y libre de armamentos nucleares," son parte integrante central de una estrategia global de lucha por la paz. Procuran favorecer la confianza mutua y la seguridad colectiva, de modo de evitar un escalamiento de la presencia de las grandes potencias en zonas pasibles de disputa hegemónica.

Quisiera señalar diversas iniciativas en la que participamos como fue la Comisión Sudamericana para la Paz, la Seguridad Regional y la Democracia, creada en abril de

1987 que tempranamente planteo la propuesta de crear una Zona de Paz en América del Sur.

Los gobiernos latinoamericanos impulsaron la creación de la Unión de Naciones Suramericanas que ha avanzado en la elaboración de políticas comunes de defensa y la Comunidad de Estados Latinoamericanos y Caribeños (CELAC), como organismos que hoy representan a "Nuestra América" para resolver conflictos e impulsar políticas comunes de desarrollo. De esta manera, en 2014, América Latina y el Caribe fue declarada como "Zona de Paz" en la histórica Declaración de la Habana de la CELAC, luego de fuera imposible realizarlo para todas las américas en el marco de la Organización de Estados Americanos en la Conferencia de Ministros de Defensa de las América del 2012, donde tanto Estados Unidos como Canadá, se opusieron a esta iniciativa.

Y esa oposición no es casual, el Reino Unido ha consolidado una base militar en las Islas Malvinas en el Atlántico Sur, que representa una presencia injustificada y desproporcionada extra OTAN que amenaza la seguridad regional. Esta amenaza es reforzada por la presencia de submarinos a propulsión nuclear, con capacidad de portar armamentos nucleares que violan tratados internacionales que establecen que esta zona debe estar desnuclearizada.

En suma, los tratados internacionales y regionales que postulan objetivos de prohibición de armamentos, desarme, zonas de paz, son instancias que disponen de un conjunto de instituciones y reglas, que aportan a "balizar" el camino para la resolución pacífica de los conflictos, no obstante presentan según los casos, debilidades y limitaciones en su capacidad para intervenir en la resolución de conflictos para que actores estratégicos con capacidad de incidencia y de veto, acepten participar en soluciones cooperativas y de desarme.

Frente a esta situación es indispensable el protagonismo de los Pueblos para reforzar el cumplimiento de esos Tratados, así como para ampliar e incorporar otras iniciativas complementarias y convergentes en favor de la paz, el desarrollo con justicia social y la democracia. Tenemos varias experiencias en este camino:

La encíclica *Pacem in terris*, del Papa Juan XXIII planteaba que: Los pueblos viven bajo el temor por las continuas guerras, conflictos armados en diversas regiones del mundo y el aumento de las armas nucleares que ponen en riesgo la vida de los pueblos y el sistema planetario y hace un llamado a la conciencia de los pueblos para exigir urgentemente "que cese ya la carrera armamentista que, de un lado y del otro—reclama que las naciones que las poseen las reduzcan simultáneamente, que se prohíban armas atómicas." El Papa Juan XXIII señalaba esto en 1963, debemos preguntarnos que se hizo en estos años y donde está la humanidad en el presente. El Foro Social Mundial, ha sido un faro para enfrentar las políticas neoliberales, los tratados de libre comercio y el accionar del sistema financiero internacional y las grandes corporaciones transnacionales, la carrera armamentista, todos ellos responsables del sometimiento y explotación de nuestros pueblos. Desde allí se gestó la esperanza de que "Otro Mundo es Posible" para el desarrollo de numerosos movimientos populares.

Frente al desafío del cambio climático, existen instancias de coordinación como las que convocó el Estado Plurinacional de Bolivia, donde movimientos sociales de todo el mundo, explicitamos con claridad que el problema del cambio climático, es la vigencia de un sistema de expoliación y depredación que amenaza hoy la supervivencia del planeta. Está plataforma ha renovado esperanzas por el "Buen Vivir," esto es otras formas de desarrollo adaptadas a nuestras realidades.

También podemos destacar las propuestas de las Centrales Sindicales del mundo, por la Democratización de la Energía, donde se avanza entre urgencias cada vez más crecientes, en el reconocimiento del acceso a la energía como derecho humano, a la vez de desarrollar fuentes alternativas de generación de energía limpias y renovables en la búsqueda de otros modos de producción y desarrollo.

La Campaña por la Abolición de las Armas Nucleares galardonada el presente año con el Nobel de la Paz de 2017, constituye un excelente ejemplo de una iniciativa gestada desde la sociedad civil, que articula con gobiernos dispuestos a liderar un Tratado de Prohibición de Armas Nucleares. Aunque los principales países que disponen de armamento nuclear se opongan a la prohibición, el Tratado señala el derrotero a seguir y contribuye a presionar para que avancen tratados multilaterales de reducción y supresión de estas armas de destrucción masiva.

Los pueblos tenemos nuestras instancias de diálogo y coordinación, podremos tener diferencias dada la pluralidad de expresiones que se manifiestan en las sociedades civiles de cada país, pero en general nos ponemos de acuerdo.

El desafío principal, es cómo potenciar formas de cooperación, iniciativas de desarme cuando las potencias dominantes no hacen más que provocar, herir y expoliar a los pueblos del mundo. Y en particular la principal potencia, EEUU a quien se le asigna el liderazgo del multilateralismo, aparece hoy día embarcada en iniciativas de provocación permanente y, diríamos en nuestro barrio, "pateando el tablero" de los organismos multilaterales para rediseñarlos más aún a su imagen y semejanza.

Asistimos recientemente a una escalada de amenazas entre Corea del Norte y Estados Unidos. El preocupante desarrollo de armamento nuclear y misiles de largo alcance por parte de Corea del Norte, como la creciente intervención de EEUU en maniobras militares en la región asiática, ha llevado al actual presidente de los Estados Unidos a plantear la amenaza de destrucción total de Corea del Norte. Que la mayor potencia del planeta amenace con el exterminio de un país, representa una gravedad inusitada que altera y amenaza todo el orden de convivencia gestado desde Naciones Unidas.

Frente a esta situación varios Premios Nobeles hemos llamado al Diálogo pacífico entre los Estados Unidos y Corea del Norte, solicitando al secretario general de las Naciones Unidas que se despliegue una estrategia proactiva de negociaciones, para trabajar en acuerdos de no agresión que congelamiento de ensayo nucleares y no realización de ejercicios militares, entre otras medidas que permitan construir acuerdos de paz y eviten escaladas de amenazas y agresiones.

El sistema multilateral presenta dificultades de regulación de los conflictos, cualquiera sea el tema que aborde. Las luchas por la protección de los derechos de las personas y de los pueblos, la defensa del medio ambiente, los procesos de desarme y la justicia requiere multiplicar del protagonismo de los pueblos en todos los terrenos posibles. Los resultados no están asegurados, pero si no lo intentamos podemos terminar siendo cómplices de un orden globalizado que bajo nuevos ropajes persiste en mantener un desorden de injusticias institucionalizadas. Los desafíos hacia dónde va la humanidad está en la decisión de los pueblos en dejar de ser espectadores y asumirse como protagonistas y constructores de su propia vida y de su propia historia.

Note

1. Cf. *Pacem in terris*, http://w2.vatican.va/content/john-xxiii/en/encyclicals/documents/hf_j-xxiii_enc_11041963_pacem.html.

8

Will Human Beings Survive Another Century?

Muhammad Yunus

Nuclear weapons have been around for many years, but this has become an issue of enormous concern because of the kind of political sound bites that the world has been hearing in recent times. Some national leaders have been taunting each other about their nuclear capabilities in language that sounds like two kids fighting over the quality of their toys. They seem to remain oblivious about the potential deaths of millions of people if these toys are activated. Dark clouds are gathering around us each day through reversal in the political directions in important countries, making the world increasingly more nervous.

Bad experiences that we have gone through over hundreds of years helped us generate enough sanity to create institutions to help us bring nations together and overcome mutual fears. Organizations such as the European Union were conceptualized and put in practice, overcoming centuries of animosity, violence, and killings. Then suddenly, a reversal took everybody by surprise when the Brexit vote happened. It was a rude shock to see one nation decide to break away from the journey of getting close to each other. This tendency is not limited to one area of the world; it is spreading. We see the same isolationism emerging out of other elections. It comes in the form of building physical and legal walls to isolate a country from the rest of the world. This is a very negative political direction in contrast to the earlier collective dream of building a global village.

This has immediate implications for weapons of mass destruction, particularly nuclear weapons. I am not an expert on nuclear weapons, and I do not wish to know how many thousands of nuclear warheads are waiting to be called into action at the push of a button. No matter how many they are, they are more than enough to destroy this world many times over. To me, this is an extreme form of insanity. What we are dealing with is not a political issue; we are dealing with human insanity of absurd proportions. Some leaders appear to race against each other to demonstrate who is more insane than others in their league.

We can easily detect how inconsistent we are in our behavior when we talk about achieving the Sustainable Development Goals by 2030 in one breath, and then aggressively promote nuclear weapons in the next breath. We express our determination to create a wonderful world and simultaneously confirm that we do not care whether there will be a world left or not; all that we are obsessed with is achieving only one outcome, being the "winner," whatever it takes.

We work hard to uphold the Paris agreement on global warming and painstakingly design timelines to achieve it before we reach the point of no return. While the world is desperate to protect the planet, some countries generously allocate money for refurbishing and enlarging their nuclear stockpile to destroy everything in seconds.

Some leaders do not see any inconsistency between these two goals. I cannot explain it in any other way but to see it as an extreme form of insanity. The important question before us is to decide whether we want to continue this insanity. We need to convince the whole world that human civilization cannot continue this insanity.

Yet instead of slowing down, this insanity is growing. It is growing from two sides. First, from the political side, which is taking a sharp wrong turn, it is showing signs of becoming inward-looking. When you become self-centered, you see the rest of the world as a threat. You tend to deal with it with firepower.

The second side is the economic side. Because I have been working with poor people, particularly poor women, many people ask me what I think are the causes of their poverty. My experience says that poverty is not created by the poor people; it is created by the system around us. Unless we fix the system, poverty is not going to disappear. So the solution to poverty is in fixing the system. There is nothing wrong with poor people; they are as good as anyone else.

I give the analogy of a bonsai tree—if we pick the seed of the tallest tree in the forest and plant it in a flowerpot, we will only get a tiny tree out of it, probably not more than 2 or 3 feet in height. It is a cute little tree, exactly like the one in the forest, but a tiny replica. Why does it not grow taller than this? The explanation is very simple. There is nothing wrong with the seed, just that it was never given the base that is required for it to grow. Poor people are bonsai people; there is nothing wrong with their seeds, but society simply never gives them the space to grow as tall as others. The economic system that we have built causes poverty. If we fix the system, there will be no poverty.

I have tried to demonstrate repeatedly how the system went wrong, and what damage the economic system has done to us. For example, it is designed as a process to create a continuous flow of wealth to concentrate at the top, in fewer and fewer hands.

Now we are told that eight people in the world own more wealth than the bottom 50 percent of the world's entire population. Four billion people's wealth is equal to the wealth of eight people! We are told that this concentration is getting worse every day. Next year, we may hear that two or three people own more wealth than the bottom 50 percent of the population. Concentrated wealth can be visualized as a huge mushroom that keeps on growing, and is owned by fewer and fewer people. The stem that hangs from this growing mushroom is getting thinner and thinner.

The stem represents the wealth of the remaining 99.9 percent of the world's population. Should we accept anything that creates such a phenomenon as an economic system, or dismiss it as a mockery of an economic system? But in reality, we seem to be going along with it. This is another form of insanity. Because we got used to living in an environment of insanity, we seem not to notice it. On one hand, we appear not to see any harm in the extreme monopoly of economic power in the hands of a few persons in half a dozen countries; and on the other hand, we do not seem to mind monopoly of power to destroy the whole world in the hands of half a dozen leaders in a half a dozen countries.

The problem of economic insanity began with the wrong interpretation of human beings in economic theory. The capitalist system assumes that human beings are driven by personal interests—in other words, human beings are selfish beings. I find it hard to accept this interpretation. Real human beings are not exclusively selfish beings, as the theory claims. They are a combination of selfishness and selflessness. By interpreting human beings as exclusively selfish beings, the theory succeeded in making people believe in it and behave accordingly. In real life, people behave as if they are fitted with glasses with dollar signs to make them see only one thing: money.

But if we interpret human beings as both selfish and selfless within the theoretical framework, the whole capitalist system becomes completely different. It will then have two kinds of businesses: the existing profit-maximizing businesses built on the basis of our selfishness, and another kind of business built on the basis of selflessness—business to solve people's problems. This I call social business, something that does not exist in business theory today.

In selfless business, the entrepreneur will not have any intention of making any personal profit. The company will make a profit, but the profit will stay with the company, to expand after the entrepreneur gets his or her investment money back.

In a selfish business, you want to make lots of money, but in a selfless business, you only think about bringing benefits to other people without paying any attention to your personal gain. If we can introduce social business idea to the world, we can have a better and balanced world for all of us.

Another vital area where the capitalist system went wrong is that it assumes human beings are born to be job seekers, that they must work for somebody else, as if a job is the sole destiny of human beings. This, too, is a wrong interpretation of human beings. Human beings are independent entities; every individual is a go-getter, an entrepreneur—that is what our history shows. It is in our DNA. We should tell our young people that they are born to be entrepreneurs. The least we can do is to tell all young people as they grow up that they have two options in life: they can choose to be job seekers or choose to be job creators. They should prepare themselves for whichever option they choose. Today, they are not given any such option.

If we accepted this interpretation that every human has the capability of becoming an entrepreneur, our whole economic system would change completely. The wealth concentration that we see would slow down, or even reverse itself, if enough young people became entrepreneurs. They would no longer be mercenaries making other people richer and richer, providing fuel for wealth concentration. Instead, they would become wealth owners themselves. They would become creative participants in the economy. With wealth becoming more widely distributed, politics would tend to get cleaner. The core of politics has to change in a way that everybody can participate in it effectively.

There is another emerging issue in this context: artificial intelligence. We are being told that soon factories, businesses, and offices will not need workers to run them. Instead, intelligent machines will run them. What would be left for humans to do? We are told that the masses of unemployed human beings that it would generate could have decent lives with a universal basic income. We are told that in the next twenty-five years, artificial intelligence will reach a level of intelligence equal to that of humans. In the subsequent twenty-five years, it is not unlikely that intelligent machines would have one thousand times more intelligence than human beings. At that point in time, human beings will appear to be as intelligent as rats on the scale of human beings and actual rats today. The machines will outsmart human beings with ease. They will decide whether they need human beings on this planet, and in what role. Even if they find a role for human beings, it is likely not to be a dignified one. Whatever role we may hope to play in that world would definitely not be the role supersmart machines would have in their mind. They may quickly realize that human beings are a dispensable nuisance.

We have another bit of insanity attached to this issue. We are so busy in the race to create superintelligent machines that we have forgotten to create any universal social watchdog to make sure there are strict guidelines to follow while we develop these technologies—such as, they will bring no harm to people physically, mentally, socially, and economically, and will do no harm to the planet.

I see one common thread behind all this insanity: the basic flaw in our greed-based economic system. To address this once and for all, we must redesign our existing unsustainable economic system, putting our human values of empathy, sharing, and caring at the center of all our activities—economic, political, and social—and creating a new civilization based on these values. If we do not do this, it is not unlikely that we—all of humankind—will disappear within a century.

9

What the International Campaign to Abolish Nuclear Weapons Can Offer for the Future Work of Nongovernmental Organizations

Beatrice Fihn

When we started negotiations earlier this year in March, His Holiness sent a message to the conference that said in part: "We need to ask ourselves how sustainable is a stability based on fear, when it actually increases fear and undermines relationships of trust between people?"

How sustainable is a stability based on fear? Fear has guided global relations, and human relations, for over seventy years. The powerful create nuclear weapons to control the world, but it is clear that weapons have controlled us. They have guided the steps of geopolitics, pinned leaders into corners, and weighed down ideals and thoughts about humanitarian law—human rights—with words like "deterrence" and "détente." The massive nuclear arsenals are a relic of a time when men, mostly men, foolishly believed that never-ending escalation, a dangerous balancing act, could secure peace. Through these decades, people of faith have been a consistent light, a constant voice pulling us back from the brink of annihilation, a steady guide out of this prison of fear that we have created. And this pope and his predecessors have continued to appeal to hope in the face of this fear, light in the face of darkness, life in the face of death. So who better to lead us out of the reliance on weapons of mass destruction than the pope and people of faith? Along with His Holiness, we have also had strong support from many bishops, including the US and European Catholic bishops, who said the indiscriminate and disproportionate nature of nuclear weapons compels the world to move beyond nuclear deterrence, when we will finalize the treaty this July.

But it was not just church leadership. Throughout this work, some of the most fearless people I have ever known have been the women of the Church. These women have been fierce advocates for disarmament. And I see actually many people nodding at this, and I think we all know: do not cross the sisters. They will not be stopped in their efforts to hasten the end of our nuclear nightmare, they are not afraid to challenge the laws of man while serving a higher calling, and their courageous actions for so many decades have challenged and inspired us. Also, the faithful have guided us and have pointed us the way to hope when we had been drowning in doubt. And now, with this historic treaty off in the distance, we can actually see the end of nuclear weapons. Men harness the power of physics to create these weapons, but we have harnessed the light of faith, the power of people, to stand against them.

It has been seventy-two years since the United States unleashed what Harry Truman called a rain of ruin. And though we are celebrating how far we have come this year, what we have achieved, we recognize the very present and real threat of nuclear weapons. In fact, we see it on Twitter, above all places, where rain and ruin have become fire and fury. And this reality makes clear the urgency of our shared mission, and we will never be safe with a stability based on fear. We will never be safe as long as nuclear weapons are a bargaining chip. We will only find safety when these weapons are gone, and the way we will get there is through the prohibition of nuclear weapons. And this is why I can caution all states to follow the leadership of the Holy See and sign and ratify this treaty. A globally binding treaty is not the final step in our journey out of nuclear darkness, but it is the beginning of the end.

Today, I made a humble request of Pope Francis that I now extend to all of you. On December 10, in Oslo, Hiroshima survivor Setsuko Thurlow and I will accept the Nobel Peace Prize—it is actually awarded on that day every year, and it happens to fall on a Sunday this year—and somebody might be busy on that day. I asked today the Holy Father to lead the global Catholic community in praying for the end of the threat of nuclear weapons, and I ask the same of you. And let the prayers of the people around the world on December 10 appeal for peace and call on leaders to join the Holy See to sign and ratify this treaty. Because the dark shadow of nuclear weapons has spread across seven decades of human history. I am convinced that through the actions of people everywhere, led by leaders like Pope Francis and leaders like the people at this conference, we will end the domination of nuclear weapons over humanity. We will stand against fire and fury by harnessing the power of people and the power of solidarity.

10

Nukes, Land Mines, and Killer Robots

Jody Williams

Insanity. I was thrilled to hear Muhammad Yunus talk about insanity. I have found myself thinking about insanity a lot lately. I think it is insane that two men who insult each other as children would have the capacity to use nuclear weapons and destroy God knows how many millions of people. Something is deeply wrong with a system that allows this level of insanity. Why should our future, or our lack of future, be left in the hands of two men—in this case the president of the United States and the "Great Leader" of North Korea? It is insane, truly insane.

I belong to the generation that had to practice how to save ourselves if our grade schools suffered a direct hit from a nuclear bomb. Regularly, we had to get down on our hands and knees under our tiny desks and then curl into a ball with our heads on our knees and our hands protecting our heads. This, we were told, would save us from dying if "the bomb" hit our school.

Of course our teachers had not discussed the US atomic bombing of Hiroshima and Nagasaki with us and likely never considered talking about the immediate and long-term effects of the bombings. But ignorance of the United States' use of atomic weapons and our grade school "duck and cover" practicing did not make me feel secure and confident; all the practicing did was make me terrified of nuclear weapons. All of which would be coming at us from the Soviet Union, of course.

My parents did not have money. I wished they did, but not so I could buy beautiful outfits to wear to school. I wished they had money so we could build our own bomb shelter. I think that it is an insanity to teach children they should curl up in balls under their desks to protect themselves from a nuclear bomb. Or to make so many of us wish we could have our own family bomb shelters to save us from Soviet nuclear attack.

On top of all that, there was the Cuban Missile Crisis that we have already heard about many times. I vividly remember it, and in particular seeing President Kennedy on our black-and-white television set warning that we may enter nuclear war if the Soviet Union did not remove its missiles from Cuba. The stark black-and-white image of Kennedy on our TV warning us of a potentially stark future will never fade from my memory.

Listening to diplomats talk about nuclear disarmament over the years has been very irritating and especially those representing the nine countries that have nuclear weapons and, at this point, still have no intention of giving them up.[1] I have worked too long at diplomatic meetings on the Convention on Certain Conventional Weapons (CCW) in Geneva, trying to ban conventional weapons through that treaty to no avail, which is why we left the UN twice to negotiate treaties to ban land mines and cluster bombs. It was simply impossible to achieve ban treaties through the CCW. To listen to diplomats who are not in favor of a nuclear ban treaty say that they truly are working toward a ban reminds me of similar things CCW diplomats would say about banning land mines. Diplo-speak is easy to interpret, and I often found myself wondering how people could twist themselves into pretzels to appear to believe the things they would say and make us believe them, too.

If the nuclear states had any desire to ban nuclear weapons, they would be banned. They would have been banned decades ago. They do not ban them because they do not want to, period. In my case, the US cannot refurbish nuclear weapons, cannot commit trillions of dollars of taxpayers' money to modernizing nuclear weapons, and then tell us that government is really going to get rid of them some day.

A few years ago I was a speaker at a public forum on nuclear disarmament in Paris. On one panel, a French diplomat boldly stated that France would never give up its nuclear weapons because if it did, nobody would listen to it. I was stunned to hear him say, "We keep our nuclear weapons because if we didn't have them, we would be so insignificant that no government would listen to us." If that is not insanity, I do not know what it is.

I am going to talk a bit now about land mines because I was involved with helping thousands of people around the world come together under the banner of the International Campaign to Ban Landmines (ICBL), with the goal of a complete ban on antipersonnel land mines. Unlike the nuclear weapons dropped on Hiroshima and Nagasaki, which can immediately wipe out a city, land mines can kill a person decades and decades and decades after the end of a war. Because of this aspect of these indiscriminate weapons, we came to call them weapons of mass destruction in slow motion.

Also, many of us who took up the issue did so out of indignation—I call it righteous indignation. I am full of righteous indignation at injustice and inequality, and insanity, and the insanity of saying that antipersonnel landmines could be used, yet those who used them were not responsible for cleaning them up.

Apart from helping create the Mine Ban Treaty in 1997, an equally important result of our effort was reestablishing the right for civil society to push governments to do what they should do anyway. In my view, governments work for the taxpayer, and as such I have every right to stand up and push them to do what they should do on their own.

In fact, as the successful negotiations of the Mine Ban Treaty came to a close, the head of the French delegation stood up and said that it was one of the few times that governments came together and were forced to do "what we should have done anyway." She did not quite say it in words I might use because that would not be diplomatic. But importantly, she recognized the fundamental role that civil society must play in disarmament—a role that has repeatedly turned the diplomatic world on its head.

Until the powerful work of the ICBL, one would generally witness diplomats sitting in Geneva, negotiating people's future while looking at beautiful Lake Geneva against the backdrop of the snow-capped Alps. In that setting it is too easy to avoid deep thinking about the horrendous impact of weapons and war on their civilian victims. These diplomats did not have to worry about being disturbed by ordinary people putting the issue in their faces. The ICBL worked hard to put the land mine issue front and center, in their faces. Because we could not lift up the diplomatic conference room and drop it in the middle of a huge minefield, we brought the realities of land mines to the diplomats.

From the very beginning of our efforts, land mine survivors were integral to the work of the campaign. They did not want to see other people suffer as they had. They mounted a petition to ban land mines and presented 1 million signatures to the head of the CCW conference. We created a "land mine field" and put it in front of the conference room door so diplomats would have to walk across the minefield to get to the meeting. A misstep would trigger a sensor that caused an explosion. Most crossed the minefield, but some diplomats snuck in through the back door to avoid the mines.

Campaigners came together in all of our varied talents and grew from 2 nongovernmental organizations to 1,300 in about ninety countries in the space of five years. We believed, and still do, that we have the right to do things that need to be done in the world to make it better for everybody, even people whom we will never meet. We will not wait for governments to do it, because we could be waiting forever. And it was that model that Pope Francis mentioned today: civil society working with international institutions, the International Committee of the Red Cross, and governments that share the same goals to bring about change.

The model worked again with the negotiations in 2008 for the Cluster Munition Treaty. And now, with the 2017 Nuclear Ban Treaty. These successes demonstrate clearly the growth of the belief of civil society and nongovernmental organizations that we can, we must, and we will be part of determining the future of this planet that we all share. I think it is insane to leave a handful of people to make those decisions "in our names." It is also insane, in my view, that citizens do not stand up and say enough already. I will give the example of my own country, the United States. The president is one of the two people, along with North Korea's "Great Leader," who could nuke the world if their rhetoric got ahead of them and they could not pull back from launching the nuclear weapons.

In the United States, 57 percent of the discretionary federal budget goes to the military, the weapons industry, and more. And I think that does not include the trillions that will go to modernizing nuclear weapons, because much of the nuclear budget is buried in the Department of Energy. Fifty-seven percent. Why do most people silently accept that the US needs to spend all that money on "national security"?

Why do people not stand up and demand of people running for office that they explain what they mean when they proclaim their support for national security? What does that mean? Is it "I am for the right of the US to nuke somebody if it wants to"? Or does it mean "I am for the right of the US to invade countries if it wants to"? We need to know what candidates mean when they talk "national security." I think we all have responsibility as citizens here and everywhere to pay attention.

Italy is one of the biggest arms dealers in the world. And yet we sit here at the Vatican and we worry about the future; but worrying is not a strategy for change. We do little if anything in our own countries to make it different. And we have the power to do so. It has been demonstrated, as I said, with land mines, cluster bombs, and now the nuclear treaty. It can be done. It just takes a bunch of people who believe that we have the right to influence our collective future. Anything can change if you get enough people together working toward a common goal.

When we talk about the possibility of a world without nuclear weapons or any other evil, we are told that those goals are a utopian dream. What does it really mean to call the desires of a majority of people on the planet a "utopian dream"? Demeaning comments like that are meant to disempower us. If our efforts to positive change are demeaned as utopian dreams, does that not mean we are a bit crazy? Utopia is something that cannot be achieved.

Well, I totally disagree with that. It is not utopian, in my view, to refuse to accept the world the way it is and working hard to make it different. That is not utopian—it is sanity. We can make steps toward a world we want to live in, not the world as it is, and just say, "Ah, utopian; I can't do that." Anybody can do it; it is not magic. It is finding people who share the same goal, working together to make it happen as it has with blinding laser weapons, land mines, cluster bombs, and nuclear weapons.[2]

And out of this model of change came the concept of humanitarian disarmament, which had a big role in the Nuclear Ban Treaty, taking the arguments away from the security of the nation, and the security of the world, and deterrence, and saying: "Wait a minute, humanitarian disarmament." We are talking about millions of human beings that you can destroy with the push of a button. *That* is insane. We refuse to accept this, and we have continued our efforts. We are still working on cluster bombs and land mines, and now all the work that stands ahead for implementing the nuclear treaty, universalizing, dragging the nuclear states into the real work of getting rid of nuclear weapons.

On top of this work, we have launched a campaign to stop killer robots. I am sure you immediately think "drones." But killer robots, fully autonomous weapons systems, are not drones. A drone has a human being who gets to look at the target, to decide whether that target is a terrorist, nonstate actor, and then a human being pushes the buttons to kill that human being.

Today, countries are developing weapons in which no human beings make the target-and-kill decisions. It is programmed; and when released, it is the weapon and its algorithms that make target-and-kill decisions. Such machines are not moral beings. They do not "decide"; it is a computer program, an algorithm, that does the work of killing. I think that there is some moral and ethical depravity when human beings think it is OK to create weapons that on their own can kill human beings. The weapon is not at the service of human beings. Human beings are at the service of the weapon systems.

The countries most advanced in developing this weaponry are South Korea, the United States, Israel, Russia, and China. But not surprisingly, it is the US that is at the forefront of developing and deploying killer robots. And we are told it is inevitable. Nothing can be done to stop killer robots. "Inevitable" in another one of those words used to disempower people from taking action. If something is inevitable, why even bother thinking about it?

Look at advanced artificial intelligence. Certainly there are important, positive uses for robotics in the in the world today. But when it comes to making machines that can kill human beings on their own, that is, again, insanity. So we have created a campaign and we are going to use the same model as the ICBL and the other campaigns, the same kind of pressure, and we will not accept that killer robots are inevitable. Nothing is inevitable, unless you do nothing. Then it *is* inevitable.

You know, somebody like me from Vermont, a little teeny progressive state in the north of the United States, a so-called tree-hugging liberal, has often been seen as a utopian fool. Well, utopian fools are the ones who helped ban blinding lasers, ban land mines, ban cluster bombs, ban nuclear weapons—and all of this since 1995.

Again, nothing is inevitable if we get out of our comfort zones, form coalitions, and take strategic action. "Ordinary people" can and do accomplish the extraordinary. It is not that the people involved are necessarily "extraordinary"; it is that the combined talents and force of people working together for the greater good are extraordinary. And that is what we did, and it can be done again and again and again and again, and we will do it with killer robots, whether somebody wants to tell us they are inevitable or not. We will not give up. We will not give in to a world where machines can kill human beings on their own. That is insane.

I want to end with a comment reinforcing or expanding what was said earlier about hunger and conflict. The Nobel Women's Initiative is an organization of six women who received the Nobel Peace Prize. We came together to use our influence and access because of the prize to spotlight and promote grassroots women's organizations around the world working in situations of conflict.

I just came back from eight days in Guatemala, where we were meeting with Mayan women from all over the country. Some of them had to travel for 18 hours to come and meet with us, and they came to talk about what industry and development were doing to their communities—destroying the aquifer, destroying the rivers, poisoning their crops, making it impossible to grow food for their own families—in the name of development.

I again agree with Muhammad Yunus when he talked about the insanity of the economic system. That economic system will put a silver mine in the middle of stolen Mayan communal land, without consultation with the indigenous population, and poison them, burn down their villages—I have pictures—rape the women, who are often on the front line of defense of their land. That is insane. It is insane to support an economic system that allows that. We can and must work together to end all these insanities.

Notes

1. China, France, India, Israel, North Korea, Pakistan, Russia, the United Kingdom, and the United States possess nuclear weapons.
2. Blinding lasers were banned in 1995 after a joint effort by the Arms Division of Human Rights Watch and the International Committee of the Red Cross.

11

The Peace Process in Northern Ireland

Mairead Corrigan-Maguire

Northern Ireland is in a deep ethnic and political conflict, and religion plays both a negative and positive role in Irish society. This was brought home to me in the early 1970s, when a young Irish republican man told me he was in the armed struggle of the Irish Republican Army fighting a just war, and that the Catholic Church blesses "just wars." We need to throw out the just war theory, which is a phony piece of morality. Instead, we can develop a new theology of peace and nonviolence and articulate a clear unambiguous rejection of violence. Religion cannot be used to justify war or armed struggle.

There are many lessons to be learned from the Northern Irish conflict. One lesson is that violence never works—be it state, relational, or paramilitary violence or the violence of sectarianism, discrimination, or injustice. For many years these methods were used, and they plunged Northern Ireland (a country of 1.5 million people) into the darkness of death and further segregation and polarization. A light in the darkness came when, in 1976, thousands of people, 90 percent of them women, marched to call for an end to violence and for peace. They called for all-inclusive, unconditional talks—including with those using violence—insisting that we must talk to our perceived enemies, be reconciled together, and find solutions. They insisted that the UK government uphold human rights and international laws and not put aside the rights of people or use means that were illegal and counterproductive. In the first few months of this civil society movement for peace and reconciliation, there was a 70 percent drop in violence.

After a long process of dialogue and diplomacy—across the communities; between people, paramilitary groups, and politicians; mediated by the civil community and members of the clergy—eventually, a Good Friday agreement was reached, in 1998. This agreement, based on power sharing among the Unionists, Nationalists, and others, was a groundbreaking achievement in that it brought together many political parties and tackled hard issues. Unfortunately, many of the policies agreed upon were not fully implemented, and thus continue to cause dissention within our executive, assembly, and community. What could have been set up was an independent body charged with the implementation of the agreement, whose recommendations for resolving disputes would be binding on the parties. In the absence of this, the executive is obliged to address every crisis on a case-by-case basis and with no commitment to accepting recommendations to resolve the crisis.

Unfortunately, the Northern Irish executive has had many problems working on a power-sharing basis, but there is hope that as time goes on, it will adopt a more cooperative and compromising approach to working on these institutions. For many, the key to progress lies with the community where people live their daily lives. The integration of our society is very important, and integrated education, peace education, therapy, counseling, and the like will be ways in which to heal and reconcile our society. At the heart of a peace culture is a recognition that every person's life and their humanity is more important than a person's ethnic inheritance. This peace culture only develops when every citizen's humanity is valued above that of a citizen's ethnic and religious inheritance. It is where a citizen's vote is sought and cast on the basis of human worth rather than perceived inheritance or identity. Empowering local members of grassroots communities, including women and youth, to get involved in community peacebuilding, job creating, and so on will give hope and build self-belief, confidence, and courage.

Postconflict, we know how long and difficult the task before us will be. We accept this challenge to change ourselves and deepen our virtues of compassion, empathy, and love, so necessary to change our society. Seeing the person in everyone and loving and serving them will help us transcend selfishness, bigotry, and sectarianism. Deepening our relationships with family, friends, and society will keep us strong and give us wisdom and courage during hard times. In a spirit of enjoyment and enthusiasm—aware of the beauty of life, creation, inside and out—we can live each moment joyfully and celebrate the gift of being alive.

We join with everyone around the world to build a demilitarized peaceful world. We thank Pope Francis for his clear moral and spiritual leadership in calling for the abolition of the death penalty and nuclear weapons. It is an illusion that we are in control and that these weapons give us security. Above all, for any of us to harbor the thought that we have the right to use nuclear weapons and commit genocide is most disturbing. We have yet to learn the lessons of Hiroshima and Nagasaki. An apology to the Japanese people by the US government, which was responsible for the genocidal act of using nuclear bombs, will help the healing of relationships and ensure that such genocidal acts will never happen again. The policy of nuclear weapons shows that we have lost our moral compass. It is long overdue for us to abolish nuclear weapons and put resources, both human and financial, into abolishing poverty and meeting human security, as set out in the United Nations' development goals.

However, we need to do more than this. Be brave and imaginative. Join together for a common vision: the total abolition of militarism and war. We do not need to limit ourselves to civilizing and slowing down militarism (which is an aberration and a system of dysfunction), but we must also demand its total abolition. We can offer a new hope to suffering humanity. Follow the vision of the Nobel Peace Prize on global cooperation to remove the scourge of militarism and war and implement the architecture of peace based on human rights and international law.

People are tired of armaments and war, which release uncontrollable forces of tribalism and nationalism. These are dangerous and murderous forms of identity that we need to transcend, lest we unleash further violence upon the world. Acknowledge that our common humanity and human dignity are more important than our different religions and traditions. Recognize that our lives are sacred and that we can solve our problems without killing each other. Accept and celebrate diversity and otherness. Heal the old divisions and misunderstandings. Give and accept forgiveness and choose love, nonkilling, and nonviolence as ways to solve our problems.

Peace and justice are necessary, and the ways of dialogue and diplomacy must be seriously undertaken—they must be insisted upon by the international community—as shown in the Iranian nuclear deal, and as could work for a North Korean peace treaty. We can transform the erroneous mind-set that violence and threats of violence work, that weapons and war can solve our problems. Punitive policies do not bring peace.

We can take courage and confidence from the fact that the science of war is being replaced by a global science of peace based on love, harmony, and reverence for life and creation. Thank you, Pope Francis, and the Vatican Dicastery for Promoting Integral Human Development. Your work of diplomacy, mediation, and fearlessly speaking truth to power, whatever the cost, gives hope to all humanity.

PART IV

Diplomats

12

The UN Conference to Negotiate a Legally Binding Instrument to Ban Nuclear Weapons: A Debate

Rose Gottemoeller, Thomas Hajnoczi, and Jorge Lomónaco

Rose Gottemoeller

Let me start by talking about NATO's essential mission. I quote from our founding documents: "NATO's essential mission is to ensure that the Alliance remains an unparalleled community of freedom, peace, security and shared values, including individual liberty, human rights, democracy and the rule of law." This mission, the role of extended nuclear deterrence and the Alliance's long-standing commitment to arms control, disarmament, and nonproliferation, form an important backdrop for our debate this afternoon. I recall the substance of discussions we had when I visited the Vatican in my previous position in 2014 and 2015. We spoke at that time about the changing security environment, achievements in the arms control and disarmament field, and the Nuclear Non-Proliferation Treaty (NPT), to which all NATO members are signatories. It is my honor to be back at the Vatican today in a different capacity, and once again to exchange views on the security environment, deterrence, and how arms control, disarmament, and nonproliferation contribute vitally to our security. The purpose of this session is to discuss efforts at the United Nations to ban nuclear weapons. I am not here today simply to criticize that initiative. Every right-thinking person and every right-thinking organization, including NATO, wants a world without nuclear weapons, period. The issue is how to get there without jeopardizing international peace and security.

Some of you will know that the North Atlantic Council, NATO's highest decision-making body, released a public statement on this issue in September. Such statements are rare and an indication of how seriously the Alliance takes this debate. That statement made clear, and I quote, that "the Alliance reaffirms its resolve to seek a safer world for all and to create the conditions for a world without nuclear weapons." The statement also emphasized the Allies' strong commitment to full implementation of the NPT as a tried-and-tested mechanism for achieving that goal in a pragmatic and verifiable manner. NATO's concern is that the Ban Treaty will not contribute to the elimination of nuclear arsenals. Instead, the treaty risks undermining years of steady progress under the NPT. Importantly, the Ban Treaty disregards the security conditions and nuclear challenges that we face, most prominently today, the emergence of nuclear weapons and long-range missiles in North Korea. Let me speak about the profound link between nonproliferation and extended nuclear deterrence.

In essence, the US nuclear umbrella made a nuclear nonproliferation treaty possible. It gave US Allies and partners in Europe and Asia the confidence to put aside their own nuclear weapons research and to become non–nuclear weapon states under the NPT. Extended deterrence dispelled John F. Kennedy's prophecy that with nuclear weapons in so many hands—countries large and small, stable and unstable, responsible and irresponsible, scattered throughout the world—there would be no rest for anyone, no stability, no real security, and no chance for effective disarmament. Effective disarmament did follow in the wake of the NPT, with the United States and USSR both destroying the Cold War excess of nuclear weapons that they acquired. From a high of over 32,000 warheads in 1967, by 2015 the United States was down to fewer than 5,000 warheads. Five thousand is still too many, I repeat this again and again, it is still too many, but we have reduced. Nevertheless, we must continue to press forward.

And I would say as well, to respond to Mohamed ElBaradei's confidence comment, that we have not reduced reliance on nuclear weapons. You just have to look at the numbers, and you must recognize that both the United States and the Russian Federation have reduced reliance on nuclear weapons in our nuclear strategies. I have already made the case for sticking with the NPT, which has abundantly proved its value. Let me spend my last few moments saying what more we should be doing, both the international community and indeed the NATO Alliance, to carry this agenda forward.

The first thing that we can do is to seek to address the underlying conflicts that drive nations toward nuclear weapons. As the NATO secretary-general, Jens Stoltenberg, recently said in Asia, are we doing enough to resolve tensions on the Korean Peninsula, in South Asia, in the Middle East? I think all our countries can do more, and indeed the international nongovernmental community can do more.

The second thing we need to do is to work harder on disarmament efforts between the United States and the Russian Federation. The United States, my own country, has reached out to Russia to reestablish strategic stability talks and address what the United States has determined to be Russia's violation of the Intermediate-Range Nuclear Forces Treaty. In February 2018 the United States and Russia will achieve the central limitations of the New START Treaty, bringing the number of deployed nuclear warheads to 1,550 on each side. For comparison, just consider that when the first START Treaty entered into force in 1994, there were approximately 12,000 deployed nuclear warheads in each strategic arsenal.

Now, and I stress this point again, we must consider what to do next, but I will not brook the notion that there has been no progress in nuclear disarmament, because there has been significant progress. Now, let us figure out what to do next. We also need to close available technical and practical pathways to nuclear weapons.

Mohamed ElBaradei noted this point, and I think it is extraordinarily important. We must renew our efforts to strengthen nuclear safeguards, working together with the International Atomic Energy Agency. We must negotiate a Fissile Material Cut-Off Treaty; we must work on practical disarmament efforts, such as the International Partnership for Nuclear Disarmament Verification; and we must try to bring the Comprehensive Nuclear-Test-Ban Treaty into force.

The security challenges we face are diverse and evolving, but I am optimistic about the future. Otherwise I would not have this job, otherwise I would not have had my previous job, and believe me, I never would have tried to sit down and negotiate the New START Treaty with the Russian Federation. But, you know, the Catholic Church puts a great deal of emphasis on faith, hope, and charity. The greatest of these is charity, or love, it is said in the Bible, but honestly sometimes I think the greatest of these is hope. So, to end, I want to invite you all to come to NATO headquarters; talk with the men and women whose job it is to see, understand, and respond to the dangers that the Allies face every day; and work with us to achieve lasting peace, security, and a nuclear-free world for all of us.

Thomas Hajnoczi

The fact that we are here together shows the Catholic Church's continuing commitment to ridding the world of the scourge of nuclear weapons. Already in 1963, through the encyclical *Pacem in terris*, the Church unambiguously and unreservedly rejected nuclear weapons. It has stood firm ever since. I am particularly grateful for the important attention and support His Holiness Pope Francis has shown for the cause of nuclear disarmament on a number of recent occasions.

Today, Austria and many other states have come to take the same position. This congruence of views has become manifest in the new Treaty on the Prohibition of Nuclear Weapons (TPNW), adopted at the United Nations Headquarters in New York last July with the affirmative votes of 122 states. I congratulate the Holy See for being among the very first to have signed and ratified this new international legal instrument.

As the head of the Austrian delegation to the negotiations on the new treaty, I am delighted about the opportunity to share with this distinguished audience some firsthand impressions and thoughts about that historic diplomatic process, and about the result which it has delivered.

First, a few remarks on the process. Before the adoption of the TPNW, multilateral nuclear disarmament negotiations had not progressed for more than twenty years. The single most important factor to change this unsatisfactory state of affairs became the international discussion of recent years about the catastrophic humanitarian impact of nuclear weapons. In 2013 and 2014, a series of dedicated conferences hosted by Norway, Mexico, and Austria went a long way to raise awareness about, and mobilize action on, this issue. Much of the credit here goes to civil society, as the world was recently reminded by the excellent decision to award the

Nobel Peace Prize this year to the International Campaign for the Abolition of Nuclear Weapons.

One of the facts brought to light in the course of the humanitarian discussion was that in one way or another, even a single nuclear explosion would affect everybody. The risk of it actually occurring is significant. And there is no such thing as a limited nuclear war. The current crisis around the nuclear and ballistic missile program of the Democratic People's Republic of Korea (North Korea) has made everybody very much aware of the grave danger we all are facing.

As everybody would suffer from the use of nuclear weapons, everybody has to have a say on them. For the negotiations, this meant that only a fully democratic process would be acceptable. They were based on a mandate from the United Nations General Assembly. They were open to all UN member states on equal terms. A decision was made to extend the same status to the Holy See and to Palestine. Nobody was granted a right to veto decisions of the conference against the will of the majority. Reflecting the important role of civil society in nuclear disarmament efforts, the participation of nongovernmental organizations was encouraged as much as possible, as was the participation of relevant international organizations, the International Committee of the Red Cross, and others. The result was an open, transparent, and inclusive process based on exceptionally broad international support, both on the state and civil society levels.

The process led to a text reflecting a significant convergence of views among a large and diverse group of negotiators. As a consequence, the most abhorrent category of weapons of mass destruction has finally been outlawed under international law, as have already been the other categories of these weapons for a long time. What is more, the TPNW creates the necessary basis for the elimination of nuclear weapons and the attainment of a world free from this scourge. The negotiators took care and succeeded to make sure that the new instrument is fully in line with the existing international nuclear disarmament and nonproliferation regime, with the NPT at its center. Specifically, the TPNW promotes implementation of NPT article VI relating to nuclear disarmament.

Of course, the adoption of the new treaty is only the beginning of a long journey. In particular, we are absolutely aware that a nuclear-weapon-free world cannot be achieved without the cooperation of the states actually possessing these weapons. Unfortunately, the reactions of these states to the new treaty so far have shown that the necessary political will to engage is not yet there. I promise, therefore, that Austria will continue to actively seek dialogue with these states, as well as with all other states, in order to broaden the common basis for taking joint further steps in the future in the pursuit of a nuclear-weapon-free world.

It seems to me that where political will is lacking, this is mainly because of the persistence of the view that nuclear deterrence is necessary for security. This is a proposition that is indeed incompatible with the TPNW, and which the supporters of the latter therefore reject. For good reason; not only does the example of the majority of states currently already belonging to nuclear-weapon-free zones, or renouncing nuclear weapons on a national level, like Austria does, demonstrate that security without nuclear weapons is possible. The abhorrent humanitarian consequences of any nuclear weapon use, and the unacceptable risk of nuclear war, suggest that security without nuclear weapons is even stronger, more rational, and more sustainable than reliance on nuclear deterrence. We must also not be blind to the fact that nuclear deterrence is working at cross purposes with nuclear non-proliferation. As long as some states cling to nuclear weapons for themselves, there will always be others that want them. North Korea is a case in point, a veritable security dilemma, from which the TPNW shows a way out.

It is striking to read again how many of the arguments just made have already been put forward much more eloquently in the encyclical to which I referred at the beginning of my remarks. In closing, let me remind delegates, therefore, of the conclusion John XXIII drew from his observations. According to him, the fundamental principle upon which peace is based in today's world must be replaced by an altogether different one, namely, the realization that true and lasting peace among nations cannot consist in the possession of an equal supply of armaments, but only in mutual trust. This is a daunting task that still stands before us today, as it did in 1963. It seems to me that if we want to survive, we have no other choice but to finally face it.

Jorge Lomónaco

It is a pleasure to share this panel with two colleagues whom I respect a lot, with whom I work a lot, often disagree, and often conspire. This is the nature of our relationship, but above everything else it is respect, tremendous respect for each other. I would divide my remarks into three parts: a little bit of background, because we need to understand where we are coming from, the jigsaw puzzle analogy—and I will get to that—and the way ahead. On the background, we heard from previous speakers the importance of the Humanitarian Initiative in building up momentum for the Ban Treaty.

So I fast-forward to the Seventieth UN General Assembly two years ago, which was very important—a key moment in my view—not only because it was the seventieth anniversary of the bombing of Hiroshima and Nagasaki, so carrying a lot of symbolism, but also because it was a crucial moment for the process. At this assembly, a group of countries presented, including us and some others, four resolutions, four legs, and I would like to spend a little bit of time describing briefly these four. Thomas described a little bit of that. The Humanitarian Initiative resolution was about bringing hard facts, scientific evidence, into the General Assembly, but it was also about the numbers, 159, so we were building numbers. The second one was the Humanitarian Pledge, which has been referred to by Thomas as well, which contained the political commitment to do something about the facts and the evidence that we had before us. The third one was the establishment of the open-ended working group, which was the vehicle, following up the commitment into practice. The fourth one, which is not as often talked about, was the ethical imperatives of a world free of nuclear weapons. And I would like to refer to it in particular, because it was about the moral dimension of the task before us, and it was inspired by Pope Francis. And a major change in the Church's doctrine, moving from condemning the use of nuclear weapons to condemning the very existence of nuclear weapons. I would invite you to look into that resolution, go straight to the operative part, where the General Assembly declares: "Given their indiscriminate nature and potential to annihilate humanity, nuclear weapons are inherently immoral." I think it is very important to see that was the moral dimension of this process. No wonder the Holy See was the first state to ratify the Ban Treaty, a true reflection of its commitment.

Now let us move to the jigsaw puzzle. The main criticisms of the Ban Treaty are: that it will not eliminate a single weapon; that it oversimplifies nuclear disarmament; and that it skips phases and steps. Well, the Ban Treaty was never supposed to eliminate weapons. That was never the intention. So if that is the criticism, the criticism is accepted. It was never meant to be the ultimate nuclear disarmament measure, the end of the process. It was meant to make a contribution, if you like, a step-by-step approach. Well, quite a worthy step, I would say, a step worthy of this conference and a step worthy of the Nobel Peace Prize, and congratulations to the International Campaign to Abolish Nuclear Weapons for that. Like a jigsaw puzzle—and I believe that nuclear disarmament and a world free of nuclear weapons are a jigsaw puzzle—where we need to place pieces. And only when this jigsaw puzzle is complete, will we enjoy a world free of nuclear weapons. The NPT is a big piece, and it is already in place, and we are very proud of it. The Comprehensive Nuclear Test Ban Treaty (CTBT) is another very important piece. I will argue that the Ban Treaty is yet another piece that fits into this puzzle, and rightly so. But there are very important pieces missing: a Fissile Material Cut-Off Treaty (FMCT), an elimination system, a verification mechanism, and so on, and so on—so we still need to work. The Ban Treaty is not only an important piece but a piece that offers a crucial element—that is, the stigmatization of nuclear weapons. Thomas already referred to how other processes have gone through first prohibition and then elimination. Slavery, for example, and other human-created scourges.

So, like a jigsaw puzzle, everyone has a different system to build a puzzle. Not everybody puts in the same pieces at the same time. Some people sometimes put one piece here and then follow with others, but a different person will do otherwise. So that is the main difference that we have. We all understand, as Thomas said, that one essential piece for that puzzle is a prohibition. The major disagreement, and I would say the only disagreement, is the order. Some of us believe that the piece had to be in place now. Others believe that it had to come later. But that is the only difference, because we all agree that a prohibition is essential.

Now the way ahead. At the risk of disappointing some, I would argue that the time has come to end the polarization between the two counts, pro and against the Ban Treaty, and find common ground to move on. Discussions and conversations over the past years have concentrated on the Ban Treaty, either in favor or against. It would seem that after the adoption of the treaty, the temptation to concentrate discussions on it remains. I believe it is time to move on. We have the Ban Treaty;

let us talk about what to do next, instead of complaining about the past. We have two choices, in my view: to use the remaining three years before us to complete the review cycle of the NPT, with some criticizing the Ban Treaty and others defending the Ban Treaty; or, as I argue, to work on a common agenda. So the challenge is which agenda. During the open-ended working group, the participants were divided generally into two groups, not of equal size, but two groups. On the one side, a much larger group of countries promoting, insisting on a Ban Treaty. During the open-ended working group, participants were divided generally into two groups, not of equal size, but two groups. On the one side, a much larger group of countries promoting, insisting on a Ban Treaty. On the other, a smaller group of slightly more than twenty countries that called its position the "progressive approach." The so-called progressive approach consisted of a list of long-sought disarmament and nonproliferation measures. Nothing new, really. Consequently, there was no disagreement on the measures themselves but rather on the fact that the progressive approach group offered them as an alternative not as a supplement to the Ban Treaty.

In the end, the open-ended working group recommended the launching of negotiations and the Ban Treaty was eventually adopted, but as a recognition to the support of the measures put forward by the progressive approach group, they were included in an annex to the report of the open-ended working group. I was planning to go through them today but in order to save time, I will just mention a few to illustrate what kind of measures we are talking about. They include more transparency, an FMCT, the entry into force of CTBT—you know, the same measures that we have been talking about for years if not decades. I would argue that now we need to concentrate our work on these measures, which clearly supplement the Ban Treaty and have enjoyed support from most for some time. The question then is whether all nuclear possessor states would be willing to finally undertake these measures. So the ball is again in their court.

13

Beyond Nuclear Deterrence: Transforming the US-Russian Equation

Alexei Georgevich Arbatov

There is a commonly accepted view that nuclear weapons have saved humankind from a third world war during the last seventy-two years after their immense destructive power was demonstrated at Hiroshima and Nagasaki in August 1945. The main argument boils down to the fact that such a war did not happen during the age of domination of nuclear deterrence in the international strategic and political environment.

Only God knows whether this is true. There is no equation between "during the time of" and "as a consequence of." The debate on this subject has been going for decades, and neither point of view can be irrevocably proved. However, it should be noted that during the whole century between the Battle of Waterloo in June 1815 and the catastrophe of August 1914 there was no large-scale war despite the absence of nuclear weapons, just like during the hundred and fifty years between the Thirty Years' War of the seventeenth century and the sweeping Napoleonic military campaigns of the early nineteenth century.

Be this as it may, there are serious reasons to suggest that nuclear deterrence will not serve as a factor in preventing regional and global war in the decades to come. There are at least three considerations supporting this assumption: (1) the new US-Russia and Russia-NATO political and strategic confrontation in the Euro-Atlantic zone; (2) expanding nuclear multipolarity, superseding former bipolarity; (3) the development of advanced military technologies and innovative strategic concepts for their employment.

After 2014 the possibility of nuclear war once again returned to relations between Russia and the West. That seemed unthinkable only a few years ago, to say nothing of the decades since the end of the Cold War in the late 1980s, when Europe looked to be at its most secure in the one and a half thousand years since the collapse of the Roman Empire. The tense standoff between Russian and US-NATO armed forces over Ukraine—and in the Baltic, Black Sea, and Arctic regions—created a threat of fast escalation of any local armed conflict and even accidental collision to a large-scale war. To some extent, similar conflicts may erupt between China and the United

States or its allies in the Western Pacific over Taiwan and disputed islands, and the jurisdiction of territorial seas.

Due to the absence of mutually recognized dividing lines of "quasi-frozen" conflicts in Ukraine, Georgia, Azerbaijan, and Moldova, a new armed clash may suddenly erupt and draw Poland, the Baltic states, Turkey, and Romania—together with the rest of NATO—into a war with Russia. Even in peacetime, large-scale military exercises of Russian- and NATO-armed forces close to each other create a threat of collisions and accidents between ships and aircraft, with an accompanying risk of escalation.

A direct military conflict between Russia and NATO in Eastern Europe, the Baltic, or Black Sea would provoke an early use of nuclear arms by any side that considers defeat otherwise unavoidable. This probability is exacerbated by the fact that tactical nuclear and conventional systems are co-located at the bases of general-purpose forces and employ dual-purpose launchers and delivery vehicles of the navy, air force, and ground forces.

If the Intermediate Nuclear Forces Treaty were to collapse, and if the deployment of new medium- and shorter-range missiles in Europe by any or both sides were to become a reality, the prospect of early nuclear use and a consequential prompt escalation of nuclear strikes from theater to strategic level would be much more probable.

For most of the decades of the Cold War, the nuclear setting was largely bipolar: the two superpowers possessed about 98 percent of the world nuclear arsenal. During the last quarter-century after the Cold War, world nuclear arsenals have been reduced numerically by about 80 percent, primarily on the account of the United States and Russia. At the same time, the number of nuclear-armed states increased from seven to nine, and the proportion of Russia and the United States combined decreased to 90 percent or even 80 percent.[1] However, much more important is the growing political role, independence, and self-assertiveness of China and the third-nuclear-armed states. All of them are involved in regional conflicts; some are unstable domestically, while Russia and the Unites States cannot control regional crises as they could in the past.

Of the nine nuclear-armed states, seven envision nuclear first use in their doctrines, official declarations, and actual operational planning. The two exceptions—China and India—have apparently been revising their no-first-use stance in recent years. Any serious military conflict in South Asia, the Far East, or the Middle East is prone with a high probability of turning nuclear, with catastrophic regional and even global consequences.

The next cycle of the nuclear arms race would no longer be a US-Russian bilateral enterprise, but will involve China, India, Israel, and North Korea, and may lead to the expansion of the nuclear club to include Iran, Turkey, Saudi Arabia, South Korea, Japan, Taiwan, and other nations. Nuclear proliferation would be the easiest environment in which international terrorism might gain access to nuclear weapons or explosive devices.

A serious reason for concern is the development of most advanced weaponry and military technologies related to the revolution in command-control-information systems, long-range precision-guided cruise and future hypersonic missiles, drones, artificial intelligence, and space warfare and cyber warfare. These technological developments and operational concepts erode the traditional delineation between nuclear and conventional arms, offensive and defensive systems, and regional and global classes of dual-purpose weapons.[2]

Nowadays the US-Russian strategic nuclear balance looks very stable, and neither party is concerned about the threat of a disarming nuclear attack.[3] And yet, paradoxically, limited or selective nuclear strikes are again considered possible, and not necessarily leading to a massive exchange. Such concepts are encouraged by the upgrading of the accuracy, yield variability, and enhanced command-and-control flexibility of the new vintage of nuclear arms.

Another troubling notion is the concept and system of "conventional deterrence," which envisions conventional long-range, high-precision strikes against the opponent's nuclear forces and command-and-control systems. Although conventional attacks on hardened targets would not be effective, most soft strategic forces' sites would be relatively easy to destroy. A strike against missile warning radars and satellite control sites would "blind" the leaders of the two superpowers and entail a high probability of nuclear retaliation.

Such concepts are as artificial as they are dangerous. If presented in a crisis to a cocky, inexperienced, and strategically uneducated leader, they could become a recipe for disaster. They are the most dangerous innovations of contemporary military strategies, with a high probability of a catastrophic nuclear escalation.

Neither of these threats could be addressed by enhancing nuclear deterrence. To deal with them requires serious steps far beyond nuclear deterrence by the United States, Russia, and other influential nations.

The first step is to apply a more concerted effort to peacefully settle Europe's ongoing conflicts, foremost in Ukraine. If the Minsk agreements are not implemented two years after their conclusion, they must be supplemented with effective enforcement mechanisms, including large UN peacekeeping operations.

The scale of military exercises of Russia and NATO should be reduced on a mutual basis and separated geographically. Confidence-building and transparency measures (Vienna Document, Open Skies Treaty) should be expanded, and the US-Soviet accident avoidance conventions (of 1972 and 1989) should be enhanced and put on a NATO-Russian footing.

Second, the Intermediate Nuclear Forces Treaty must be preserved and mutual US-Russian accusations of noncompliance should be addressed and removed through diplomacy under the strong political guidance of the leaders of the two powers. They should also initiate without further delay the talks on a follow-on START Treaty with the goal of achieving substantial reductions of strategic arms, and addressing other issues of disagreement. The movement in this direction would be conducive to enhancing nuclear nonproliferation and eventually engaging other nuclear-armed states in the arms control process and conflict resolution agreements.

Third, Russian and American leaders should reconfirm that "nuclear war cannot be won and must never be fought," as their predecessors proclaimed in the early

1970s and late 1980s.[4] In this reconfirmation, they should be joined by the leaders of the other seven nuclear-armed states.

But this is not enough—additional principles must be added to this philosophy. These common principles, for example, should include the recognition that any use of nuclear weapons, however limited, is inherently escalatory and should be excluded from the great powers' strategic relations.

Finally, it should be also acknowledged that weapon systems blurring the line between nuclear and conventional operations are destabilizing and should be subjected to limitations and/or confidence-building measures. Expanding defensive systems to reduce each side's vulnerability to rogue states should only be based on their agreements.

Whether nuclear deterrence in the past has saved the world, it will not provide such assurance in the future. Human civilization, which is sustaining its security with the ability to exterminate itself during several hours of nuclear warfare, does not deserve the title "civilization." It is high time to find an alternative source of insurance.

Notes

1. Along with the "Big Five," Israel, and South Africa, nuclear arms were acquired by India, Pakistan, and North Korea, while South Africa abandoned them in 1992. The uncertainty of 80 vs. 90 percent stems from the absence of official data on China's nuclear forces, while the range of experts' estimates stretches from about 300 to 1,000 deployed warheads.
2. Those are systems capable of delivering nuclear or conventional munitions.
3. Russia is only concerned about the United States' "prompt global strike" conventional systems and conventional ballistic missile defense, and the United States is only concerned about Russia's tactical nuclear arms.
4. Quoted from Ronald Reagan's 1984 State of the Union Address.

14

International Diplomacy and International Security Issues

Izumi Nakamitsu

On behalf of Secretary-General António Guterres, I would like to thank His Holiness Pope Francis and the Holy See for hosting this conference. This event further illustrates your commitment to a world free from nuclear weapons and continued efforts to achieve it. The Holy See was one of the very first to sign and ratify the Treaty on the Prohibition of Nuclear Weapons. It has been a consistent moral voice for our shared goal to rid the world of these devastating weapons.

I would like to recall Pope Francis's words to the General Assembly in 2015: "An ethics and a law based on the threat of mutual destruction—and possibly the destruction of all mankind—are self-contradictory and an affront to the entire framework of the United Nations."

I have been given a very broad topic, "international diplomacy and international security issues," to reflect on. In my humble attempt to address this subject, I would obviously like to try to drill down and focus on the role of the disarmament and nonproliferation regime as a diplomatic pillar that reinforces international peace and security, given my position as UN high representative for disarmament affairs.

Disarmament in History

But before that, let me put this into a historical context by briefly touching on centuries—or in fact, millennia-long efforts in human history to regulate the conduct of individuals, groups, and states in war. These efforts date back to the time of the Old Testament or Hindu Mahābhārata, and continue throughout human history.

More recently, since the mid-nineteenth century, the international community has sought to progressively develop the law of armed conflict in parallel with rules to prohibit or restrict specific weapons that cannot be used in conformity with humanitarian principles.

Some of the earliest international disarmament agreements established universal norms against weapons that cause superfluous injury or unnecessary suffering, or whose use would be repugnant to the conscience of humankind. These included prohibitions in 1899 on bullets that expand or flatten in the human body, in 1907 on poison and poisoned weapons, and in 1925 on asphyxiating, poisonous, or other gases and bacteriological methods of warfare.

The role of disarmament as an essential element of contemporary international peace and security stems largely from the terrible human consequences that resulted from two world wars, including the first and thankfully only uses of nuclear weapons in conflict at Hiroshima and Nagasaki.

Since the end of World War II, this humanitarian imperative has also been clearly linked to the broader mechanism for peace and security. The adoption of the United Nations Charter saw a clear evolution in the international security architecture: use of force by a member state is only allowed for self-defense and under the collective security arrangement defined in Chapter 7 of the UN Charter—an agreement that, admittedly, has not been fully implemented. Disarmament is part and parcel of this international peace and security architecture.

Put simply, the purpose of disarmament is to prevent and end wars, and save lives—to ensure both state and human security, security for all. This is why disarmament was a founding principle of the United Nations. It is reflected in both the UN Charter, which calls for "the establishment and maintenance of international peace and security with the least diversion for armaments of the world's human and economic resources," and for a system to regulate armaments, and the very first UN General Assembly resolution, which sought to eliminate "atomic weapons and all other weapons adaptable to mass destruction."

Unfortunately, despite this historical underpinning, recognition of the importance of disarmament to the prevention, mitigation, and resolution of conflicts has somehow diminished in recent years. As we see international tensions continue to rise, I would like to appeal to all of you to help reaffirm disarmament as a core part of our international agenda, and to underscore our common goal of creating a more peaceful and prosperous planet that is safer and more secure for all.

Disarmament in the Twenty-First Century

Secretary-General António Guterres has described today's geopolitical context as a complex, interconnected web of new and old conflicts. These conflicts have precipitated gross violations of international humanitarian and human rights law, and have forced millions of people from their homes. It is a world of heightened international tensions and inflamed regional conflicts.

In such a fractious and uncertain world, many voices contend that the time is not ripe for disarmament and that weapons provide security. There is an insinuation that disarmament is a utopian dream.

I believe that quite the opposite is true. In a fractious and uncertain world, more than ever we need disarmament as a diplomatic key to unlock the door to peaceful solutions. In fact, we have historical evidence to this effect: the Partial

Nuclear Test Ban Treaty came into force only a year after the Cuban Missile Crisis, followed by Nuclear Non-Proliferation Treaty several years later—both at the height of the Cold War.

Our work is based on a strong recognition that peace and security do not depend on the dangerous and destabilizing accumulation of arms but on a commitment to shared norms, dialogue, transparency, and confidence in one another's actions. As the only existential weapons ever created, nuclear weapons must remain our priority, and we must work tirelessly toward a world free of them. However, disarmament, nonproliferation, and arms control of all types of weapons are core elements of both conflict prevention and conflict resolution—whether we are talking about small arms and light weapons, explosive weapons, heavy artillery, or chemical weapons. And the problem of weapons pervades every peace and security crisis across the world, from violent crime, to civil war, to terrorism, to interstate conflict.

Three Roles of Disarmament in the Maintenance of International Security

Next, I would like to dig a little deeper and discuss three aspects of how disarmament can help maintain international security today: first, the role of disarmament and nonproliferation norms in international security; second, the fundamental role of disarmament and nonproliferation in diplomatic strategies to prevent, mitigate, and resolve conflict; and third, a future outlook of international security and the role of disarmament and nonproliferation diplomacy.

Norms in International Security

First, the role of norms. The disarmament and nonproliferation regime is a constellation of instruments designed to promote a plethora of norms. These norms are aimed at preventing or diminishing the impact of armed conflict or violence. Today, such norms are vital. The threat of nuclear war is not an abstract one. Armed violence is on the rise, and complex and brutal civil wars continue to force civilians to flee. In many countries, attacks using improvised explosives now kill and injure civilians and combatants more than any other type of weapon. When explosive weapons were used in populated areas, civilians accounted for 92 percent of casualties.

Much of this carnage is the result of the inappropriate use of weapons, inadequate regulations on arms transfers, and poorly implemented controls on military stockpiles that have led to the widespread availability and misuse of weapons. This includes a growing illicit arms trade that fuels civil wars, violent extremism, and criminal violence. As was recognized in Goal 16 of the Sustainable Development Goals, the illicit arms trade also prevents socioeconomic development.

In recent years, the international community has sought to create the norms that will address these concerns. Two instruments are of particular relevance. First, the Arms Trade Treaty, which entered into force in 2015, seeks to create a norm of vigilance in the global arms trade against, for example, the diversion of weapons to armed groups or the use of weapons for the perpetuation of gender-based violence. Second, since the turn of the century, governments have agreed to improve national small arms laws, import and export controls, and stockpile management, and to engage in cooperation and assistance under the Programme of Action to Prevent, Combat, and Eradicate the Illicit Trade in Small Arms and Light Weapons in All Its Aspects, which creates a strong norm against the diversion of weapons to the illicit arms trade.

As recognized by this conference, perhaps the most important norm that has been developed over the last seventy years is the norm against the use of nuclear weapons and the pursuit of their total elimination. This is a norm based on a shared understanding of the catastrophic—probably existential—consequences of a nuclear conflict.

A range of instruments underpins this norm, but the load-bearing wall is the Nuclear Non-Proliferation Treaty (NPT). The NPT's near universality, verifiable nonproliferation safeguards, and binding commitments to disarmament mean that it has made an invaluable contribution to international peace and security, and the shared norm that is the goal of a world free of nuclear weapons.

The NPT, which opened for signature this past September, creates additional norms for subscribing states. It effectively places nuclear weapons on the same level as chemical and biological weapons, and further emphasizes the terrible humanitarian consequences of the use of even one nuclear weapon.

However, for norms—even universally held ones—to be continually effective they must be actualized through full implementation of all commitments by as many states as possible. Without constant tending they can, and do, decay. Despite the good progress made since the end of the Cold War in arsenal reductions, risk mitigation, and the decreasing role of these weapons in national security doctrines, the threat of a nuclear conflict appears to be growing.

Almost every day, we hear dangerous rhetoric about their utility and calls for enhanced roles in national security doctrines. Modernization campaigns in every single nuclear-armed state are provoking a qualitative, if not quantitative, arms race. The historic arms control treaties of the 1980s and 1990s are being eroded by claims and counterclaims of noncompliance. Beyond the New START Treaty, there are no envisioned negotiations on strategic arsenal reductions.

The collective will for nuclear disarmament has devolved into an increasingly acrimonious debate. In such an environment, it is critical to keep intact the norms contained in the NPT and the practical security benefits they provide. As we head toward the 2020 Review Conference, states' parties must inject a sense of urgency into finding common ground and ensuring the continued vitality and centrality of the NPT.

Key to this is remembering that nuclear disarmament and nonproliferation are two sides of the same coin: they are mutually reinforcing. In this context, it should be understood that failure to achieve concrete progress in nuclear disarmament will undermine the NPT. There is an urgent need for practical measures for irreversible, verifiable, and universal nuclear disarmament.

The need for actualization and implementation of norms is true across the disarmament and nonproliferation spectrum. For example, 130 states have signed up to the Arms Trade Treaty, but only 92 have ratified it so far. If this treaty is to be effective, it needs universal buy-in and application.

Disarmament as Prevention and Resolution of Conflict

My second point relates to the role of disarmament in conflict prevention and resolution. I have already mentioned the Sustainable Development Goals, but it is worth highlighting that they underscore a long-understood concept: disarmament provides the breathing space to build confidence, engage in broader dialogue, and pursue socioeconomic development.

Arms control provides an avenue for dialogue even—perhaps especially—during times of heightened tension. We should not forget that it was groundbreaking treaties such as the Intermediate Nuclear Forces Treaty and the Treaty on Conventional Forces in Europe that laid the groundwork for the peaceful end to decades of the Cold War.

More recently, the Joint Comprehensive Plan of Action on the Iranian nuclear issue has provided an example of how a tense international security issue can be resolved through direct engagement and a shared commitment to dialogue and cooperation in good faith. A sustained commitment by all participants to the agreement remains critical, not only for its continued viability, but also for the efficacy of diplomatic solutions to questions of peace and security.

The current crisis in Northeast Asia is a clear example of how disarmament will play a central role in bringing about a negotiated solution. The UN secretary-general has stood firmly with the international community in condemning the nuclear weapon and ballistic missile activities of the Democratic People's Republic of Korea (DPRK; North Korea). However, it is a crisis that can only be resolved by a political solution based on a comprehensive and sustainable settlement through diplomacy. Any such solution will need to involve the DPRK's nuclear weapons and ballistic missile programs and the will of all parties to achieve sustainable peace. As I have said before, only by finding solutions at the negotiating table can we prevent a potential humanitarian disaster.

The Future Outlook of International Security

The third and final role I want to highlight is how disarmament diplomacy can help prevent future international security crises. In his address to the General Assembly in September, Secretary-General Guterres said, "Technology will continue to be at the heart of shared progress," but also that the "dark side of innovation" is a threat we must confront, and one that has "moved from the frontier to the front door."

Advances in technology are transforming the world in a way not seen since the Industrial Revolution. However, the same innovations transforming transportation, health care, and manufacturing also have either military applications or can be repurposed for malicious intent. The potential use of these innovations for military or even malicious purposes could have significant implications for international peace and security.

Technological innovations with such potential implications include enabling technologies, such as machine learning or information and communications technology. Others are dual use, such as biotechnology and additive manufacturing. And there are specific weapons technologies, such as new types of long-range precision delivery vehicles and armed unmanned aerial vehicles. Taken together, these innovations could increase the likelihood of armed conflict by lowering the threshold for conflict, reducing decision-making time and the window for escalation control, and increasingly placing civilians in harm's way.

In the near term, the security implications of this suite of technologies will have ramifications for international humanitarian and human rights law. The portability, availability, and relative ease with which much civilian technology can be repurposed for malicious ends all raise serious proliferation concerns, including for nonstate actors.

There is much we do not know about the peace and security implications of emerging technology, especially its combined effect. But we need to start asking questions now about how we can mitigate potential risks in ways that do not stifle innovation or the equitable transfer of technology for peaceful purposes and sustainable development. And we need to ask these questions of an increasingly diverse range of actors, including the private sector—the drivers of this technological renaissance.

I have done my best to illustrate how disarmament, as a central pillar of international diplomacy, can help resolve security crises. The global climate is rife with discord, and diplomatic solutions are needed more than ever. If we are to move forward together, we should heed Pope Francis's exhortation that the common destiny of humanity "demands the pragmatic strengthening of dialogue and the building and consolidating of mechanisms of trust and cooperation."

15

The Role of International Diplomacy and International Organizations

Thomas Stelzer

Yesterday, being addressed by the Holy Father, first as a group, he was not talking to the converted, but, with his unequivocal confirmation that even the possession of nuclear weapons is to be condemned, he gave us a new sense in our own individual mission to go out and help him advocate, meaning help him understand, our friends, our people, what is in our shared interest. And then, of course, when Pope Francis addressed each one of us, individually—shaking our hands, looking into our eyes, sharing his generosity, his gentleness, his authenticity—this was extremely inspiring. Let me just say the Mass this morning emphasized all of that, you know, looking up to the image of the Holy Spirit and having time to reflect on the message of Francis yesterday was just a very strong experience. And Cardinal Turkson, may I just add a little. Your metaphor of sharing peace when we greet each other was very beautiful. I just would like to add one little sentence here. I come from a country, Austria, where we do not say to each other "good day" or "guten tag" when we greet each other, but we say "grüß Gott," "greet God." We greet in each other the imperfect image of God. I think this is a very strong sharing of the message of peace.

    Now, I am not going to talk about the United Nations and its role in disarmament. Izumi Nakamitsu has already spoken on this comprehensively. There is nothing to add. She has even given to us a very concise wrap-up of thousands of years of disarmament efforts. And when I listened to this, I had these images rising in me, which have been perpetually repeating, the walls of Jericho, the walls of the Middle Ages, walls that could not prevent the First World War, iron curtains to keep people in countries, fences to keep the victims of globalization, which is benefiting all of us so much, out of our countries. So the walls and fences are a metaphor for our own insecurity, and I think it is quite appropriate here in Italy to share with you an impression I had a few years ago of the contemporary Italian composer Luciano Berio, with one of his two operas, which he called the *azione musicale Cronaca del luogo*. When I heard the first performance of this opera at a Salzburg festival in 1999, the musicians—it was the Salzburg Felsenreitschule, which is a vertical wall, with niches—the singers were behind the wall, you could not see them, but the musicians, the fifty soloists, were spread out in the niches of this wall. While I was sitting there listening to this music, I felt this wall disappear, and I thought I understood the secret of walls. For me this was a very formative moment, because I think much of what we have been discussing has a relation to walls. Why do I say this? You know, I am not here as ambassador to Portugal, I am here because I have spent most of my life on global issues, trying to understand and help and include, and when we speak at the United Nations of inclusive sustainable development we want to bring people to the center. What is the reason for most of the conflicts today? In my analysis, every conflict is the consequence of unsustainable imbalances. When imbalances become unsustainable, a crisis evolves. And one of the reasons why the world is in this state today is because we keep people away, out, we build walls, we impede access.

You know, there was this argument today that the money invested in nuclear disarmament could be used much better for other issues, more productive issues. When I was on the first committee at the beginning of the 1990s, this was a time of hope, the end of the Cold War, and we were talking about the peace dividend, what we could do with the peace dividend. It is true, the investments went down for a few years, and then they leveled out, and they have been rising ever since, starting in about 1995. For the past fifteen years, they have been rising and then flattening out again. And today, we spend about $1.7 trillion a year on investments in armaments. To just put this into a little bit of a balance, the combined official development assistance, official development aid, that we give to help people rise out of poverty and create opportunities to take their own life into their own hands—and to live up to their own expectations and aspirations, to invest in families and in houses—the combined money for that today is $142 billion, a fraction, not even 10 percent. You know, even if you add remittances, the money that migrant workers send back, which is normally used in a very targeted way to help develop, that is another $230 billion, so not very much. So we cannot talk about money.

I think much of what we talk about is not rational. Politics is perception. We perceive our reality. We cannot win people over with rational arguments, unless we are able to create a narrative that people can buy into, where they recognize what is in their own interest, come on board, join our integrative platforms. So it is exactly what Jody Williams has told us: bring people, mobilize them, give them a target, give them hope, make them understand that you can create a better world. Unless we achieve that, we will not achieve our goal of, in our case, nuclear disarmament. And we cannot talk about conclusive or less or more conducive situations. Of course the United Nations institution succeeding is a very fragile and very complex issue, and a conducive environment very much helps. But in disarmament we have been having so many good opportunities already. How many more do we want?

When I remember April 2009, President Barack Obama in Prague, we were all enthusiastic, how much better could it go? The president of the United States stated that "America's commitment was to seek the peace and security of a world without nuclear weapons." You know, we let the moment pass. I mean, this is a very special group of people, of course, consisting of some of the most accomplished disarmament experts, but also of some of the most accomplished disarmament motivators and practitioners. Some of them were even awarded the Nobel Peace Prize for their achievements. But we do not reflect a consensus outside this room. I have to say this. There is a strong consensus in this room, not on everything, but there is a strong consensus that we have to do away with nuclear weapons as a strong contribution for future peace. Now we have different views on how far we are and what we have achieved, that we can discuss. But there is a strong consensus in this room on what we want to achieve. This consensus does not exist outside.

The UN General Assembly does reflect very well the evolving consensus on many different topics, on pretty much every topic in the world. And the first committee, the main committee for disarmament and security, deals with nuclear issues and reflects the lack of consensus in the world. In fact, of the six main committees of the General Assembly—the first one dealing with international peace, security, and disarmament—is the one with the least consensus, and the nuclear question, for example, this year in the ongoing General Assembly there were fifty-eight resolutions up for decision in the first committee, twenty-two on nuclear issues. On sixteen resolutions, there was no consensus, they had to be taken for a vote. Only six resolutions on nuclear issues could be adopted without a vote. This was the same as last year. Last year also, six resolutions could be adopted without a vote and nineteen had to be taken for a vote. So this reflects the lack of consensus out there in the world.

Now, what can we do? What can public diplomacy do? What can the United Nations do? What can international organizations do? When I talk about the United Nations, I am not only talking about the Secretariat Building, the glass palace, I am talking about the United Nations family, which consists of many different organizations, funds and programs, specialists, agencies, and other related organizations. I had the privilege to serve for five years as the secretary of the Chief Executives Board. The secretary-general meets twice a year with the twenty-seven heads of the United Nations system to talk coordination on the big issues. Disarmament was not an issue there. It has never been taken up by the UN family. At the Chief Executives Board meeting, disarmament was given a fixed place, about 15 minutes, Mohamed ElBaradei remembers very well, the director-general of the International Atomic Energy Agency got a slot there to share with us developments because the topic was not discussed in the United Nations, because there was no UN initiative on disarmament. Initiatives take place in state conferences, where there is no consensus. But there is no UN consensus as such to drive disarmament, there is no real conference on disarmament, no Rio+20. These conferences don't take place in the disarmament field, because there is no consensus.

Now, how can we build a consensus? How can we contribute to that? The United Nations is an intergovernmental organization, where governments come together and work on topics and in a best-case scenario somebody identifies a lacuna, and has a great idea, builds up a strategy, and then talks to his friends and then listens to adversaries, builds a group of people who support him or her, builds a big initiative, and in a best-case scenario helps people to buy into the initiative and creates a shared ownership of the outcome in the end. This is very important, to share the ownership.

But the United Nations Charter does not speak to the governments of the world. It speaks with the peoples of the world, who go far beyond the governments of the world. Of course, in an ideal democracy, governments reflect the people and their will, but we are not discussing democracy or philosophy here. There is a consensus in the United Nations that it can only be viable and successful if we bring in its constituents, who go beyond the governments. So many times governments work very hard to achieve norms in the United Nations. They come up with conventions, great conventions, they are full conventions. Many of them become deadwood afterwards, because governments are so exhausted after all the efforts that come with the convention that they lose interest, and it is not their convention. There is no buy-in, and there is no accountability; nobody holds them accountable to do what they have promised to do. And this is the role of constituents, this is the role of civil society. Civil society, with topics that go beyond the four-year electoral cycles of governments, which have long-lasting topics, which can mobilize, which can hold politicians accountable to their promises during the electoral periods, and vote them out, or bring them back afterwards. But for that, we need a mobilized, informed civil society. And this is why I very much appreciate your role, which is indispensable.

So, I think we were able to contribute to this understanding of the United Nations, that the United Nations needs to become more and more an integrative platform, to bring together governments of course, as an intergovernmental organization, but also academia, civil society, and business. We are doing that, you know, in different forums. We need all these constituents to produce a shared outcome afterwards, that people do not drop their conventions once they have achieved them, but also see the need to implement them.

Let me come back to the walls. When you look at the world today, there were so many very interesting statements and questions about its status. There are some things that are quite striking and that call for action. In the policy paper here, the concept note of the conference, in the first paragraph there is the very important notion of *Populorum progressio* "that has developed a Christian vision of the human person introducing the concept of integral human development and also considering development as a new name for peace." Peace is not only the absence of war, this is fragile; peace is something active, something we have to struggle for every day. It is well worth fighting for. But I am a pragmatist. When I look around in the world, where do we have peaceful situations? Every year they come up with this scale of the most and least peaceful countries, and when you look at these countries, what is striking is that the most peaceful ones have the most integrated societies, with the highest level of economic, social, and political integration. The least peaceful countries are the most polarized; they are not able to release and integrate tensions. And this means, as a conclusion, that sustainable peace can only be built on sustainable inclusive development. And this is what the 2005 summit outcome said. There is no peace without development, there is no development without peace, and both have to be based on human rights, on the respect for the human being. This is the reason why we do all that.

Now, how can we achieve that? At the end of the 1990s, when you looked at the distribution of global wealth, the image resembled an Italian moscato glass, a very flat spumante glass. Today, world wealth has multiplied, but the image is a fine line, there is no glass, it is a fine line. Muhammad Yunus referred to that. You know, eight or ten people who own half the world's wealth, this is a metaphor. The reality is—and this is again my subjective experience, of one with a life in global issues—our weak point is the lack of capacity to integrate, to bring people together; we keep them out.

There are millions and millions of HIV-affected people who die today because we do not buy antiretroviral medicine for them, although we could. Nobody dies in the modern North. In Africa you have to line up, you have to wait until somebody in front of you dies, so that you can step in the line to have access to antiretroviral medicine and survive your HIV/AIDS infection, because you are kept out, you are not provided access to your life-saving medicine. The Food and Agriculture Organization is convinced that we can easily feed 9 billion people if we do it right. Today we have only 7 billion, but nearly 1 billion do not have food security. There are 800 million or 900 million people who do not have food security. In Yemen we are facing one of the biggest starvation catastrophes of the last decades, but we only shrug our shoulders. I could go on with these examples.

There are billions of people without access to clean water, to medicine, to decent work—a very important issue. Before Rio+20, the UN came up with a report on the social situation, because sustainable development is built on the economic, environmental, and social pillars. The economic pillar does not need any care because it is strong enough and economic development is quick. The environmental pillar is well-taken care of by civil society. The social pillar is very weak. And the report of the UN came up with a result that was totally shocking for me: more than 5 billion people do not benefit from social protection. So everything to which we are accustomed—decent, rights-based work; legal vacations; medical care when we are sick; retirement care—two-thirds of the global population does not even know what they are, and they have no access to them.

Recently, the president of the European Union's Commission said that the EU has created 8 million jobs since the 2008 crisis. I looked into that, because I thought this is great, this is striking. Hardly any of these jobs are decent; they are all precarious, one-person enterprises, which is fantastic. You know, driving Uber cars is a great thing, because you can manage your own time, or distributing pizza, until you fall off the bike, and you break your leg and you are out of work for six weeks and you have no benefits, and nobody pays your mortgage or for the school for your children. And these are the only jobs you are producing, because otherwise we have not produced jobs in Europe, and we are happy with about 1.2 or 1.5 percent growth, which is not enough. Our capitalist economic system is built on expansion, and we are just recognizing that there is no unlimited growth because there are no unlimited resources.

So these are huge challenges we have to deal with, and of course we cannot deny the future. There will be robots, there will be automated systems taking over our jobs. There will be no drivers in a few years, the buses are driverless already, the trucks are driverless already, the undergrounds are driverless. In a few years nobody will get a driving license anymore. It is going to be a move from a computer, which picks you up with an app command in front of your house and drives you wherever, which I think is fantastic to a certain extent, because we get rid of 2 billion cars, which fill parking places for 90 percent of their lifetime. We will free up all these parking places for common use. When a car picks us up, it is always useful. It is a lot of benefits, but the fallout is—what are we doing, how are people going to define their own value, after we have become accustomed, define our human value by our remuneration for the value we add to the economy? This will be over. None of us will have jobs. We are the first generation. I have small children, and, you know, I am not a pessimist, I am a great optimist, otherwise I would not be here.

Being a European, I am really impressed by the level of development we have achieved, perhaps the highest level of development in human history. We have done away with capital punishment, and we have introduced social safety networks in most of our societies. But our children are going to be the first generation in human history that cannot rely on living better than their parents. Every generation so far could rely on living better than their parents. Our children will not be able to do that, because there will be no jobs, there is no job creation. The world is growing every ten or twelve years by a billion people, and this means every year we have to create 70 million jobs worldwide just to integrate population growth. We are not creating jobs on a global level. We are losing. How are we going to provide opportunities to the people? How are state and civil society going to be able to offer a future to our children? In Europe we already have countries with youth unemployment rates of 50 percent, 60 percent, 30 percent in countries now, where we are not able to provide what is expected of the state. So what will this mean for the stability of our society, for peace?

Two things struck me yesterday. When last night I looked at many of the Facebook pages of my friends, we all of course posted our meeting with the pope. What struck me was that each face was beaming with happiness, which I think was a fantastic gift, and which also reminded me of something the Holy Father said yesterday. He referred to the teaching of John XXIII, who stated, "Unless this process of disarmament be thoroughgoing and complete, and reach men's very souls, it is impossible to stop the arms race, or to reduce armaments, or, and this is the main thing, ultimately to abolish them entirely." Reach men's souls, make us messengers of peace, make us enactors—but that we can only do if we understand the value of peace and of this great environment that will help us take this message out to the world.

PART V

International Civil Society

16

The Humanitarian Initiative as a Condition for the Ban on Nuclear Weapons

François Bugnion

I need to apologize on behalf of the president of the International Committee of the Red Cross (ICRC), Peter Maurer, who was initially invited to present this paper. He is chairing a conference of the International Red Cross and Red Crescent Movement in Antalya, Turkey, bringing together National Red Cross and Red Crescent societies from all over the world. One of the main items on the agenda of that conference is how the Red Cross and Red Crescent Movement can work to promote a nuclear-weapon-free world.

Likewise, this important conference at the Vatican seeks to further progress on nuclear disarmament, an issue that has become increasingly prominent on the international agenda, with rising regional and international tensions. This is a discussion that is both timely and urgent.

The ICRC's perspective on nuclear weapons is framed by its experience in dealing with the horrific consequences of the atomic bombing of Hiroshima in August 1945. The head of the ICRC delegation in Japan, Marcel Junod, was indeed one of the first foreign eyewitnesses to the tragedy, and he alerted ICRC headquarters with a chilling telegram: "Conditions appalling. City wiped out. Eighty percent of all hospitals destroyed or seriously damaged.... Many victims ... now dying in great numbers. Over one hundred thousand wounded in emergency hospitals."

With the help of the medical services of the American armed forces and in partnership with the Japanese Red Cross Society, he organized one of the very first relief actions in favor of the victims of the atomic bomb—an action still commemorated today in Hiroshima, although it was tragically inadequate, compared with the magnitude of the disaster.

Less than one month after Hiroshima, the ICRC launched an appeal in which the organization called for the adoption of some form of agreement prohibiting the use of this new weapon. The ICRC renewed its appeal in 1950, and has voiced its concern many times since then. Appeals for nuclear disarmament have also repeatedly been made by the International Conference of the Red Cross and Red Crescent.

The ICRC was again directly confronted with the risk of nuclear war in October 1962, on the occasion of the Cuban Missile Crisis, when the secretary-general of the United Nations requested its support in order to back his own efforts to broker a peaceful solution to that crisis which had led, for the first and only time in history, to a direct confrontation between the United States and the Soviet Union about their strategic weapons. The ICRC observed on that occasion that a nuclear war between major powers would not only disregard the fundamental distinction between combatants and civilians, military objectives and civilian objects, and would prevent any humanitarian action to provide assistance to the victims, but that it would also jeopardize the very future of humanity. Indeed, with nuclear weapons, humanity had acquired the means of its own destruction.

This, in the view of the ICRC, is part of the background against which nuclear weapons have to be assessed:

- The unspeakable suffering caused by nuclear weapons.
- The absence of an adequate response capacity to assist victims of nuclear weapons.
- The risk of global annihilation.

If we now look at the current situation, the most recent development is the adoption on July 7, 2017, of the Treaty on the Prohibition of Nuclear Weapons—an important step in the direction of nuclear disarmament. We would like to commend the 122 states that adopted the treaty. We would like to congratulate the 53 states that have already signed it, and to extend our warmest congratulations to the three states—Guyana, the Holy See, and Thailand—that have already ratified the treaty. Special gratitude should be expressed to the Holy Father and to the Holy See for their unfailing and efficient commitment toward the adoption of this treaty.

Today, perhaps more than ever before, the world needs the promise of this new treaty. The world needs the hope of a future free from nuclear weapons. Humanity cannot go on living under the dark shadow of nuclear warfare and the unspeakable suffering that would result from it—not to mention the risk of the complete annihilation of humankind. This treaty is an essential and long-awaited step toward a future free of nuclear weapons.

And it is a step that is timely. Indeed, a range of eminent security and military experts have reached the conclusion that the risk of nuclear warfare—whether deliberate, by accident, or by misreading the intentions of any other nuclear power—has today reached levels not seen since the end of the Cold War. This is profoundly disturbing and highlights that progress toward the prohibition and elimination of nuclear weapons is more necessary than ever.

In our analysis, once the treaty enters into force, it will play an important role because it reinforces the stigma against any use of nuclear weapons; it supports commitments to nuclear risk reduction; and it is a clear disincentive for proliferation.

This new treaty is firmly based on the principles and rules of international humanitarian law, such as that of the distinction between combatants and civilians, that of the distinction between military objectives and civilian objects, that of proportionality, and that of the prohibition of unnecessary suffering—namely, suffering that serves no military purpose.

Many states, the ICRC, and other organizations have long expressed serious concerns about the compatibility of the use of nuclear weapons with international humanitarian law. In its Advisory Opinion of July 8, 1996, on the Legality of the Threat or Use of Nuclear Weapons, the International Court of Justice concluded that "the use of nuclear weapons would generally be contrary to the principles and rules of international humanitarian law," although the court was unable to decide whether, even in the extreme circumstance of a threat to the very survival of the state, the use of nuclear weapons would be legitimate.

For its part, the ICRC finds it difficult to envisage how any use of nuclear weapons could be compatible with the principles and rules of international humanitarian law, even in a case of self-defense. The facts that underlie these conclusions were presented and discussed at the conferences in Oslo, Nayarit, and Vienna on the humanitarian impact of nuclear weapons. These important meetings confirmed the ICRC's assessment that nuclear weapons are unique because of their tremendous destructive power and because of the level of human suffering that their use would cause. Such use, even on a limited scale, would have catastrophic consequences for human life, health, and the environment. These conferences also confirmed that the humanitarian consequences of the use of nuclear weapons—even under the hypothesis of limited nuclear warfare—cannot be restricted to the territory of the country targeted and will inevitably make an impact on other states and their populations, because radiation and radioactive fallout know no borders.

As the ICRC learned from its experience in Hiroshima, there are no effective means of assisting the survivors in the aftermath of a nuclear detonation, while adequately protecting those delivering such assistance. It means that the majority of victims would be denied the medical assistance they would need and to which they would be entitled.

Finally, research and experience have demonstrated that the consequences of nuclear weapons are not limited in time. Not only would the survivors suffer for decades from the consequences of radiation exposure, but the consequences would also affect future generations. While in Hiroshima a few years ago, I visited the hospital of the Japanese Red Cross and saw with my own eyes Hibakusha, namely, those people who survived the atomic bombing and need regular medical attention and treatment for cancers and other diseases directly attributable to their exposure to radiation. Today, more than seventy years after the bombing of Hiroshima and Nagasaki, and thus more than seventy years after the end of World War II, the Japanese Red Cross continues to treat survivors on a regular basis.

These facts underlie the humanitarian initiative that helped bring about the Treaty on the Prohibition of Nuclear Weapons. These are the concerns that led states to consider how to advance nuclear disarmament and to take important steps to help prevent nuclear weapons from ever being used again. With this initiative and the adoption of this treaty, these states have now clearly rejected nuclear weapons on humanitarian, moral, and legal grounds. We hope that this success and momentum will be directed to ensuring that as many more states as possible sign and ratify the treaty, so as to bring it into force rapidly.

However, the work to further the elimination of nuclear weapons must also progress in other forums. Efforts to promote and implement the Nuclear Non-Proliferation Treaty (NPT) remain crucial to upholding the goal of nuclear nonproliferation and disarmament.

In this respect, we believe that the Treaty on the Prohibition of Nuclear Weapons is not only fully compatible with the NPT but that it also represents a significant step toward fulfilling existing commitments under Article VI of the NPT. Indeed, the credibility of the NPT risks being undermined unless progress is achieved toward nuclear disarmament. The Action Plan adopted by the 2010 NPT Review Conference must therefore be fully implemented. Such action would go far in helping to lead humanity closer to a nuclear-weapon-free world—a goal for which all states have expressed support.

For all these reasons, we appeal to all states that have not yet done so to consider signing and ratifying the Treaty on the Prohibition of Nuclear Weapons. No single measure could contribute today more effectively to the objective of nuclear disarmament.

This Vatican conference is a chance to help make further progress, and such progress can be made if all the spiritual and moral strengths gathered in this New Synod Hall unite toward the objective of a world free from the threat of nuclear weapons.

Action must be taken now. The risks are too high; the dangers are too real.

17

The Role of Civil Society

Susi Snyder

I speak here about the role of civil society in furthering integral disarmament, and it gives me great pleasure to talk about this, because integrating disarmament into our efforts to build just and peaceful societies is a necessary task. This conference is timely in bringing efforts for development, peace, and disarmament together in order to pursue humanitarian disarmament.

It has been interesting and empowering to hear so many varied voices of civil society, and to have the intergovernmental organizations and governments with which we work also presenting thoughtful perspectives for our path toward a world without nuclear weapons and how we might use the Treaty on the Prohibition of Nuclear Weapons to further nuclear disarmament efforts.

Civil society consists of many actors, from the business sector to nongovernmental organizations to coalitions and campaigns. In many ways, civil society is an amplification of the moral compass that is needed to guide decision-making that puts the collective good at the forefront.

Civil society gathers and galvanizes support for strong disarmament initiatives. Often driven by a humanitarian imperative, civil society works consistently to strengthen international law, to protect civilians, and to advance our human development beyond old clumsy tools of indiscriminate harm.

Civil society helps to hold our elected officials accountable for their commitments to disarmament and building a just peace. We amplify the moral imperative to act with urgency for development and disarmament. A vibrant civil society is an indicator of a healthy society.

When it comes to nuclear weapons, the voices of civil society have maintained attention and expertise on the issue for decades. Many thought the urgency to deal with nuclear weapons was lost at the end of the Cold War, but civil society kept the need for nuclear abolition in its sights. I am honored to stand on the shoulders of those who came before me, who kept the fire burning for nuclear abolition.

It is from civil society that we hear stories of what happened, and connect theoretical scenarios to actual humanity. In the words of the survivor Setsuko Thurlow:

Within that single flash of light, my beloved Hiroshima became a place of desolation, with heaps of skeletons and blackened corpses everywhere. Of a population of 360,000—largely noncombatant women, children and elderly—most became victims of the indiscriminate massacre of the atomic bombing. As of now, over 250,000 victims have perished in Hiroshima from the effects of the blast, heat and radiation. Seventy years later, people are still dying from the delayed effects of one atomic bomb, considered crude by today's standard for mass destruction.

Civil society makes sure that powerful words like these orient us toward nuclear abolition and, through civil society efforts, that we will never forget the tragedies of our past, as we work to prevent them from ever happening in the future.

The nuclear weapons discourse has changed in the last few years because of a concentrated effort by civil society, international organizations, and some governments. To shift discussion away from the false idols of deterrence and mutually assured destruction, civil society drove the question back to its very simple root: is it ever acceptable to cause or threaten indiscriminate fiery destruction?

The International Federation of Red Cross and Red Crescent Societies, and the International Committee of the Red Cross, have clearly said "No." This is never acceptable, and the use of nuclear weapons would violate the principles of international humanitarian law. I would like to congratulate the Council of Delegates of the Red Cross and Red Crescent Movement that just adopted a resolution that includes a four-year action plan supporting signature, ratification, and full implementation of the Ban Treaty.

The majority of the world's governments have taken up this question and have said loudly and clearly that nuclear weapons should never be used again, under any circumstances. The majority, 159 governments, have joined their voices in this powerful statement, and together they have elevated the question of whether nuclear weapons can ever be legitimate. One hundred twenty-two nations voted only a few months ago to finally outlaw nuclear weapons.

None of this would have been possible without the partnerships facilitated through civil society. To be effective, civil society must make strategic and tactical decisions and engage with different actors, amplifying different voices at the right times and places.

In taking forward the Treaty on the Prohibition of Nuclear Weapons and in advancing the humanitarian disarmament agenda as a whole, civil society needs to continue expanding its alliances and engaging with effective influencers. This can and does take many forms. For two examples, consider physicians who take the Hippocratic Oath to "first, do no harm" into the arena of political persuasion, and the scientists who have explored and explained the damage to our bodies caused by nuclear weapons. These partners are necessary to illustrate the urgency of change and to explain the terrifying consequences if we do not.

Mary Olson, a biologist with the Nuclear Information Resource Service, is one of these scientists. She explains: "Any nuclear explosion also emits ionizing radiation so intense that bodies are literally cooked if not shielded. Ionizing radiation exposures may also burn and produce the syndrome called 'radiation sickness.' Yet, even a single radioactive emission, so small it cannot be detected, may strike a living cell; over time, the resulting damage may become a fatal cancer. Therefore, regulators acknowledge that there is no safe radiation exposure-level above zero."[1] This evidence-based approach adds urgency to the need to prevent harm, because there is no safe exposure to nuclear weapons and the risk of use continues to grow.

The media also plays a role, which recently has been to describe the increasing risk of a nuclear conflict. Using this elevated awareness, civil society is working with partners in politics to build support for activities that might help reduce this risk.

Right now, we have an opportunity to act with urgency and possibly reduce the risk of the use of nuclear weapons. US senator Bob Corker has called for a hearing to discuss the authorization for the use of nuclear weapons, the first such hearing since 1976. This is an amazing opportunity to ask the fundamental question of whether it could ever be legitimate to use weapons that incinerate a city in a flash. It is also an opportunity to state clearly that any use of nuclear weapons is now prohibited under an international treaty.

Civil society also engages in other creative progressive efforts. One of the projects we are really glad to implement as part of the International Campaign to Abolish Nuclear Weapons is called Don't Bank on the Bomb. Through this unique project's research and publication, we publicly identify the companies behind the production of nuclear weapons.

Because nuclear weapons are not only produced by government agencies, in most of the nuclear-armed countries, private companies produce the key components necessary to use nuclear weapons. Don't Bank on the Bomb identifies the companies involved, and also names the banks, pension funds. and insurance companies that invest in them. These financial institutions are trying to make a profit by helping to build inhumane and indiscriminate weapons. We name them and actively engage with them to encourage them to end their investments. We also encourage the governments that are currently ratifying the Treaty on the Prohibition of Nuclear Weapons to include an understanding that the prohibition on production also prohibits any investment in the companies that produce them.

Don't Bank on the Bomb is also a way for civil society to play another of its necessary roles: to keep offering hope and confidence that change is possible. We make it a point to also profile those institutions that have rejected any association with nuclear weapons producers—those that have excellent policies preventing investment. It is important to always have role models.

We know from other efforts that divestment, by even a few institutions, for the same reason can have a tremendous impact on the way a company operates. Recently, two American companies decided to end the production of cluster bombs, despite the United States' failure to sign onto the Cluster Munitions Treaty. The companies said they wanted to enable European investors to engage with them again. Divestment activities are powerful, and they generate change. They are also something with which anyone who has a bank account or pension fund can engage.

Any religious community can also seize this opportunity to make sure its investments do not fuel weapons but instead facilitate sustainable development.

Hope is fueled by the opportunity to take action. These opportunities are provided by civil society globally, and they build on one another. A small success can build and grow and eventually become a world-changing event.

Gandhi may have never actually said, "First they ignore you, then they laugh at you, then they fight you, then you win," but the sentiment reflects the underlying power of continued and consistent efforts to create change for the good, for peace.

Twenty years ago, when the Treaty to Ban Antipersonnel Land Mines was signed, we witnessed the power of civil society and the potential of humanitarian disarmament. It continued with the prohibition of cluster munitions and now includes the prohibition on nuclear weapons. Civil society, working with states and international organizations, can and does harness the power to prevent unacceptable suffering and redirect energies toward building sustainable and just societies.

Civil society plays many roles. It elevates and amplifies the voices of those affected. It reframes and reshapes discussions. Civil society can move politicians to show leadership and advance policies to move mountainous agendas, at least a little bit. Civil society provides the evidence, the research, and the justification for acting to prevent harm, to disarm now—before it is too late. And civil society is creative. We come up with slogans and cheers, demonstrating in the streets, or dancing atop decommissioned missile silos. Civil society is a necessary partner in moving the abolition agenda, and through all our efforts, civil society continues to hope—hope that the goodness in every human heart will shine through the darkest of times and lead us to the light of a nuclear-weapon-free world.

Today we need this hope. The hope found in campaigns like the International Campaign to Abolish Nuclear Weapons. The hope portrayed by our partners around the world. And with this, I hope we will continue to work together to achieve nuclear disarmament and integral human development.

Note

1. Mary Olson, "Human Consequences of Radiation: A Gender Factor in Atomic Harm," in *Civil Society and Disarmament 2016: Civil Society Engagement in Disarmament Processes—The Case for a Nuclear Weapons Ban* (New York: United Nations, 2017), 26–34, https://doi.org/10.18356/52afbc66-en.

18

Reconciliation and Disarmament

Marie-Noëlle Koyara

First, I would like to say that both my delegation and I are very pleased to participate in this important research forum for world peace. This is because I come from a country that has experienced a serious crisis, one that continues to be affected by that crisis, and one that is still seeking peace. Moreover, it is an honor for us to be here in the Vatican, because in 2015, at the height of our crisis, His Holiness traveled to the Central African Republic to bring a message of love, mercy, and peace to Central Africans, and, for the first time in the history of the Church, His Holiness opened the door of mercy in our country. He invited Central Africans to rise above, to forget the problems that divide us, and, hand in hand, to seek the road to peace. I had the honor of presiding over the organization during that visit, so it means very much for us to be here.

A world without weapons, without nuclear weapons, without large- or small-caliber weapons—these are all weapons, and we know how dangerous they are for humanity. We also know what the interests are behind these arms. We know that the challenge of creating a world without weapons is a challenge that will require a lot of effort. When will we create a worldwide chain reaction, where everyone will say no? We believe that we can get there one day and that nothing is impossible when people join their hearts together to face a challenge.

Here, I would like to talk about reconciliation and disarmament, using my country—the Central African Republic—as an example, even if the Central African Republic is just like many other countries, especially in Africa, that have been through or are going through a similar crisis.

To introduce my country quickly, it is very large—670,000 square kilometers—but its principal problem stems from the fact that it is surrounded by many countries that are currently in a state of crisis, or that were in the past—countries such as Congo, South Sudan, the Democratic Republic of Congo, and Chad. And we think

---

This English translation by Paul Young, an associate professor in the Department of French at Georgetown University, is followed by the original French. —Editors.

that part of our problem also stems from the fact that the other neighboring countries that are in a crisis took refuge in the Central African Republic because it is a very welcoming country. We welcome everyone, we accept many immigrants, and sometimes these people that we welcome bring with them the problems that they have in their own countries.

The other element of our crisis is internal, and that is due to poor governance, because it is a country that is very, very rich in natural resources, and yet we have a population that is very, very poor. More than 70 percent of the population is poor, and more than 60 percent of our young people are unemployed. As you can imagine, often it is these young people who are used in armed conflicts. We live in a country that has more than 15 million hectares of farmland, and yet we still need food donations, despite the efforts that have been made in this sector. All these things have led to a crisis in our country.

The consequences of this crisis are truly manifold; we can still recall women and children who fled their villages to go live in the bush. If we think about it, we would say that people are not made to live in the bush, that the bush is reserved for animals; and yet, the crisis forces people from their villages to go live in the bush, because they seek safety. Sometimes, when they arrive in the bush they do not find that safety, because armed gangs can attack them there. It is not really possible for this population to cultivate land, because they are afraid of farming the land, and that makes them vulnerable. Not only are they afraid for their lives, but they are also faced with food insecurity, because they cannot farm. This affects at least half of our country.

Also, the consequences of this crisis have created a multitude of other crises that have not been very well managed. There have been a lot of negotiations in the Central African Republic, or in neighboring countries; there have been many meetings and discussions, there have been forums, and often people think they have reached the root of the problem. Our country has received several peacekeeping missions, and yet we wonder why, with all these different negotiations, with all these different peacekeeping missions, we still experience crises. The last one that we experienced, in 2013, was the worst in our history. Thinking about it, always within the framework of this country in crisis, we think that one solution could be disarmament.

Before reaching this solution, we decided to organize several discussion sessions. That led to a national forum, and in this national forum we drew up guidelines so that our country could return, once and for all, to peace.

Among the measures proposed, was, in fact, disarmament, which we call a disarmament of mobilization, reinsertion, and repatriation, because, among the armed groups, there are many that do not come from the Central African Republic, and this measure should also lead toward their repatriation. But what do we know?

After the program of disarmament was devised, after the country was able to mobilize resources, after having organized the constitutional referendum in the country, after having democratically elected a head of state and an assembly, we thought that with democracy and with the resources that had been mobilized, we could then proceed with disarmament and know peace in the country. But, unfortunately, after all this, we realized that the crises had become even more intense. Did we have to have armies in front of people's hearts before we could even think of a real disarmament? That is the question that we are asking ourselves.

Also, as long as we have not been able to disarm, can we hope for reconciliation? That is another question that we are asking ourselves. But, moving toward reconciliation: who should reconcile with whom?

In the beginning of the crisis, some thought that it was a sectarian crisis, others thought that it was a crisis of governance, and some even dared suggest that it was a religious, or interreligious, crisis. But really, this crisis does not have anything to do with religion, because in this country all religions have always lived together for hundreds of years. People do not just wake up one day and start attacking each other for religious reasons, so that idea was pushed aside.

Now, we know that armed groups have also been attacking the civilian population, but why? Civilians do not have weapons, and it bears noting that, despite the United Nations embargo that prevented or limited weapons, during this period the number of arms increased dramatically, especially among armed groups that had not signed any agreement—rebels. They stockpiled weapons—sometimes cheap weapons—and one could wonder, "Did this embargo have an effect upon the rebel groups?" This is a question that people are really asking themselves, and, when we see the United Nations, people wonder: "Are the United Nations really going to help us protect ourselves? With the embargo, there are a lot more weapons around!"

Surely, without the presence of the United Nations in the country, we think that we would have a catastrophic situation on our hands. But there are also limits as to what a peacekeeping mission can do. When we look at the Central African Republic, the army was totally disorganized. Now we are in the process of restructuring our national army, but restructuring this army raises problems, because the country is under an embargo and therefore we cannot equip the army with the material they need to defend the country alongside the peacekeeping missions. Young people, many of whom have been bought to be members of armed groups, do not have work because the crisis has complicated everything, and therefore it is even more difficult to create employment for these young people.

So, all this becomes a vicious cycle, and yet we need to move toward reconciliation. Programs have been started; we have started raising awareness in the population, and putting in place local committees for reconciliation both in the capital as well as in the provinces of the country. Unfortunately, these committees cannot really work, because each week we have another attack by an armed group. These armed groups have all signed disarmament agreements. Some have even taken advantage of the negotiations with Sant'Egidio, and they signed the accords to proceed with disarmament. Alongside the work of Sant'Egidio, there is also a program for African meetings that encourages these armed groups to put down their weapons and to move toward disarmament, demobilization, and reintegration—the program called DDR—but unfortunately, these initiatives have yet to bear any fruit on the ground because ten out of the country's sixteen regions experience conflict each week. Thus we are really faced with a very complex situation.

Should we reconcile before proceeding with DDR? This might have been ideal, because we must disarm hearts, put down our arms, make peace with each other, and work together to revitalize this country. But unfortunately, we have noticed that there are other, more important interests that keep encouraging these armed groups to not put down their weapons, despite all the agreements they may have signed.

We have noticed that often they can be found around the richest areas, so it appears that these armed groups are motivated by economic interests. And ultimately, we think that the crisis the Central African Republic is experiencing is due to the richness of its natural resources. So our path forward becomes complicated unless we decide upon a way to regulate the use of these resources; if armed groups are not going to put their weapons down, reconciliation will become even more complex and complicated.

So, this is the situation that this population faces, and it really requires the support of each and every person, because today it is the Central African Republic, but we have also welcomed people from neighboring countries. Tomorrow, this crisis could also affect another neighboring country, just as it might affect another country somewhere else in the world, because, it is true, the world is a small village. It is hard to know where conflict starts, or where a conflict will arrive, especially because nowadays many elements often factor into these conflicts.

Our concern today is to see concretely how we should, little by little, restructure our army, and redeploy that army in the field. If we manage to equip the army's troops so they work side by side with peacekeeping missions, there would be a distinct advantage, because many people in the army are former military, who left the service and became rebels. Sometimes these former rebels find themselves before a commanding officer, or a regular army, and yet they do not change their opinions, and come around to moving toward the idea of DDR.

So, this is a little overview of the current situation we are experiencing in the Central African Republic, a country—as I noted—both rich and poor, which today is crumbling under the weight of a crisis. Because we are a country rich in natural resources, sometimes we have the feeling this crisis was brought about by outside forces.

I would like to make an appeal to everyone, to global solidarity, so that tomorrow, the Central African people who are suffering so much now can get back on their feet, because we will evolve toward a world without arms, toward a world of disarmament, toward a world that seeks peace and serenity, so that the joy of living on this Earth that God gave us shines on every face.

La Réconciliation et le Désarmement

Avant ma déclaration, je me permets de dire que ma délégation et moi-même nous nous réjouissons de participer à ce grand forum de recherche de la paix à travers le monde. D'abord, parce-que je viens d'un pays qui a connu une grave crise, qui continue encore à souffrir de cette crise et qui continue à rechercher la paix. Ensuite, c'est un honneur pour nous d'être là au Vatican, parce qu'en 2015—au plus grave de notre crise—sa Sainteté a fait le déplacement en République Centrafricaine pour amener un message d'amour, de miséricorde et de paix au centrafricains et pour la première fois dans l'histoire de l'Eglise sa Sainteté a ouvert la porte de la miséricorde dans notre pays. Il a invité les centrafricains à passer à l'autre niv(eau), oublier tous les problèmes qui nous divisent et main dans la main cherchant le chemin de la paix. J'ai eu l'honneur de présider l'organisation de cette visite, donc pour nous c'est vraiment important d'être ici.

Un monde sans armes, armes nucléaires, armes à gros calibre, armes à petit calibre—ce sont toutes des armes—et nous connaissons les dangers pour l'humanité. Nous savons aussi quels sont les intérêts qui sont derrière ces armes, nous savons que le défi pour arriver à avoir un monde sans armes c'est un défi qui va demander beaucoup d'efforts. Mais quand nous allons cultiver une chaîne mondiale pour dire non? Nous pensons que nous pouvons un jour y arriver et rien est impossible quand les cœurs se mettent ensemble pour relever un défi.

Le temps que je devrais développer ici c'est de réconciliation et désarmement en prenant le cas de mon pays, la République Centrafricaine, mais ce cas de la République Centrafricaine ressemble beaucoup à d'autres pays, surtout en Afrique, qui connaissent ou qui ont connu cette crise.

Si je dois présenter rapidement mon pays, c'est un pays qui est très vaste—670 000 kilomètres—mais notre premier problème est dû au fait que nous sommes entourés par beaucoup de pays qui sont en crise ou qui ont été en crise: il y a le Congo, il y a le Soudan du Sud, il y a la République du Congo, il y a le Chad et nous pensons que une partie de nos problèmes sont dus aussi au fait que les autres pays voisins qui sont en crise se sont repliés en République Centrafricaine parce-que c'est un pays d'hospitalité; on reçoit tous le monde, nous recevons beaucoup d'immigrés et parfois ces personnes que vous recevez aussi entraînent avec eux les crises qu'ils ont dans leur pays.

L'autre facteur de notre crise est interne et cela est dû à la mauvaise gouvernance, parce que c'est un pays très très riche en ressources naturelles et en contraste nous avons un peuple qui est très très pauvre. Plus de 70 pourcent de la population est pauvre, nous avons plus de 60 pourcent de nos jeunes qui sont sans emploi et vous conviendrez que souvent ce sont les jeunes qui sont utilisés pour ces conflits armés. Nous avons un pays qui a plus de 15 millions d'hectares de terres pour l'agriculture, mais qui continue à vivre de dons alimentaires malgré les efforts qui sont faits dans ce domaine. Tout cela réunit a provoqué des facteurs pour amener la crise dans ce pays.

Les conséquences de cette crise sont vraiment multiples; nous avons encore un mémoire des enfants et des femmes qui ont fui des villages pour vivre dans la brousse. Souvent, quand nous sensibilisons, nous disons que les gens ne sont pas faits pour vivre dans la brousse, la brousse est réservée aux animaux ; mais voilà que la crise chasse les personnes des leurs villages pour aller vivre en brousse, parce-qu'ils cherchent la sécurité et parfois arrivant dans la brousse ils n'ont pas cette sécurité aussi, parce-que les bandes armées peuvent les agresser là où ils sont. Cette population n'a pas vraiment le potentiel pour cultiver parce-qu'ils ont peur de cultiver la terre et cela les expose—non seulement—ils ont des problèmes de sécurité pour leur vie, mais ils sont aussi des problèmes d'insécurité alimentaire, parce-qu'ils ne peuvent pas cultiver et cela concerne au moins la moitié de notre pays.

Les conséquences aussi de cette crise découlent une multitude de crises qui n'ont pas été bien réglées, parce-qu'il y a eu beaucoup de négociations en République Centrafricaine ou dans les pays voisins; il y a eu beaucoup de séances de dialogue, il y a eu des fora et souvent on pense avoir touché le fond du problème. Il y a eu plusieurs missions de maintien de la paix que notre pays a pu recevoir, mais on se demande pourquoi avec toutes ces différentes négociations, avec toutes ses différentes missions du maintien de la paix que nous continuons encore à connaître des crises et la dernière que nous avons connu en 2013 c'est la crise la plus grave de notre histoire et en réfléchissant et, comme toujours, dans le cadre de ce pays en crise, on pense que une des solutions pourraient être le désarmement.

Avant d'arriver à cette solution, le pays c'est permis encore d'organiser plusieurs sessions de dialogue à la base qui ont conduit à un forum national et ce forum national a dicté des lignes de conduite pour permettre au pays de revenir définitivement à la paix.

Parmi les mesures qui ont été proposées il y avait justement le désarmement, que nous appelons désarmement de mobilisation, réinsertion et rapatriement, parce-que parmi les groupes armés il en a beaucoup aussi qui ne sont pas des originaux et le programme doit procéder aussi à leur rapatriement. Mais qu'est-ce que nous connaissons?

Après que le programme de désarmement a été élaboré, après que le pays a pu mobiliser des ressources, après avoir organisé le référendum constitutionnel dans le pays, après avoir élu démocratiquement un Chef d'État et l'Assemblée, on croyait que avec la démocratie et avec ces fonts qui ont été mobilisées on pouvait passer au désarmement et connaître la paix dans le pays. Mais malheureusement après tout ce processus on se rend compte que les crises ont encore augmenté d'intensité. Fallait-il des armées devant les cœurs avant de penser au désarmement réel? C'est la question qu'on se pose.

Et peut-on aller à la réconciliation tant que nous n'avons pas réussi à désarmer? C'est aussi une autre question que nous nous posons. Mais aller à la réconciliation: qui doit se réconcilier avec qui?

Au début de la crise on avait pensé que c'était une crise communautaire, d'autres ont pensé que c'était une crise de gouvernance, on a même osé dire que c'était une crise religieuse, inter-religieuse, mais finalement cette crise n'a rien à voir avec la religion, parce-que dans ce pays toutes les religions ont toujours cohabité ensemble depuis des centaines d'années. Ce n'est pas du jour au lendemain que les gens vont commencer à s'agresser pour des raisons de religion, donc cet aspect a été écarté.

Maintenant, nous savons que les groupes armés attaquent aussi la population civile, mais pour quelle raison? La population civile n'a pas d'armes et ce qu'il faut noter aussi c'est les Nations Unies ont mis aussi un autre pays sous embargo, pour éviter ou limiter la sécurité des armes; mais bien que tant sous embargo c'est pendant cette période que le nombre d'armes a beaucoup augmenté et surtout du côté des groupes armés non conventionnels, c'est-à-dire les rebelles. Ils se sont beaucoup approvisionnés en armes et parfois des armes de dernière qualité et on se demande: "Est-ce que cet embargo a un effet sur les groupes rebelles?" C'est vraiment une question que la population se pose et quand nous avons en face de nous les Nations Unies la population interroge:

"Est-ce que les Nations Unies vont vraiment nous aider à nous protéger ? Puisque avec l'embargo il y a beaucoup plus d'armes qui circulent!"

Oui, sans la présence des Nations Unies dans le pays nous pensons que nous devons connaître une situation catastrophique, mais il y a aussi des limites aux interventions des missions de maintien de la paix. Et quand nous voyons le cas de la République Centrafricaine l'armée a été totalement désorganisée et c'est maintenant que nous sommes en train de restructurer notre armée nationale et cette armé qui est en train d'être restructurée a des problème aussi, parce-qu'ils ne peuvent pas intervenir parce-que le pays est sous embargo donc nous ne pouvons pas équiper cette armé avec les équipements nécessaires pour aller défendre la population au côté des missions de maintien de la paix. Les jeunes, dont une bonne partie ont été achetés pour être les membres des groupes armés, ils n'ont toujours pas d'emploi parce-que la crise a tout compliqué et donc ça devient encore plus difficile de créer l'emploi pour ces jeunes.

Donc, tout cela devient un cercle vicieux, mais il faudrait aller à la réconciliation. Des programmes ont été initiés, on a commencé à sensibiliser la population, à mettre en place des comités locaux de réconciliation—aussi bien dans la capitale que dans les provinces du pays—mais malheureusement ces comités ne peuvent pas du tout fonctionner, parce que chaque semaine nous avons encore des attaques de groupes armés. Ces groupes armés ont tous signé un accord de désarmement. Il y en a qui ont même profité des négociations avec Sant'Egidio, ils ont signé les accords pour aller au désarmement. Au-delà de Sant'Egidio, il y a aussi un programme de réunion africaine qui encourage ces groupes armés à déposer les armes pour aller vers les DDR, le programme de DDR, mais malheureusement toutes ces initiatives n'emportent encore rien sur le terrain parce-que dix régions sur les seize dans le pays connaissent chaque semaine des affrontements. Donc, nous sommes devant vraiment à la complexité de cette situation.

Est-ce qu'il faut c'est réconcilier avant d'aller au DDR? Ce qui aurait pu être l'idéal parce que nous devons désarmer les cœurs, déposer les armes, se réconcilier et se mettre ensemble pour relancer le pays, mais malheureusement, en effet, on a constaté qu'il y a d'autres intérêts plus important qui continuent à pousser ses groupes armés rebelles à ne pas déposer les armes malgré tous les accords qu'ils ont eu à signer.

On a remarqué que souvent ils se retrouvent autour des zones qui sont les plus riches—donc ce sont les intérêts économiques qui intéressent ces groupes armés et pour finir nous pensons que finalement cette crise qui la RCA connaît c'est une crise qui est due à la richesse des ses ressources naturelles. Donc, le chemin à parcourir devient compliqué si on n'arrive pas à trouver les règles nécessaires pour l'exploitation de ces ressources et si les groupes armés ne vont pas déposer les armes, la réconciliation deviendra encore complexe et compliquée.

Voilà cette situation qui connaît ce peuple et qui demande vraiment le soutien de tous et chacun et de tout le monde, parce-qu'aujourd'hui c'est la République Centrafricaine mais—j'ai dit tout à l'heure—nous avons accueilli les pays voisins. Demain cette crise peut aussi toucher un autre pays voisin tout comme un autre pays à travers le monde, parce que, c'est vrai, le monde est un petit village—on ne sait pas d'où ça commence et d'où ça peut atterrir, surtout que de plus en plus il y a beaucoup d'éléments dont tenir de compte.

Notre préoccupation aujourd'hui c'est de voir concrètement comment nous devrions arriver petit à petit à restructurer notre armée, à redéployer cette armée sur le terrain.

Si nous arrivons à les équiper pour que cette armée travaille au côté des missions de maintien de la paix, l'avantage de redéployer cette armée dont une bonne partie des ces gens sont des anciens militaires qui ont quitté le rang et qui sont devenus des rebelles. Donc, ces anciens rebelles se retrouvent devant leur chef ou devant une armée régulière, mais sans pouvoir les amener vraiment à changer de position et à se ranger pour aller vers le programme de DDR. Donc, voilà un peu cette situation que non connaissons pour l'instant au niveau de la République Centrafricaine, un pays—comme je l'ai dit—riche et très pauvres, qui aujourd'hui est en train de crouler sous le poids d'une crise qui parfois on a l'impression de croire qui est une crise emportée, parce-que c'est un pays qui a des ressources naturelles.

Je m'as appelle à la solidarité mondiale et de tout le monde pour que demain ce peuple centre-africain qui est en train de souffrir énormément puisse enfin sortir la tête parce-que nous allons évoluer vers un monde sans armes, vers un monde de désarmement, vers un monde qui va chercher la paix et la sérénité, pour qu'on lise an moins sur les visages des tous et de chacun la joie de vivre sur cette Terre que Dieu nous a donné.

19

The Risks of Nuclear War Today

Paolo Cotta-Ramusino

Nuclear weapons have been used only twice in war; nevertheless, the buildup of nuclear arsenals progressed relentlessly up until the 1980s. The number of US nuclear weapons reached a maximum of 32,000 in 1967, while Soviet nuclear weapons reached a maximum of 45,000 in 1986. Although the numbers subsequently decreased, the United States and Russia together still possess nearly 14,000 intact nuclear weapons. Taken together with the approximately 1,200 nuclear weapons possessed by the other seven nuclear weapon states (France, China, the United Kingdom, Pakistan, India, Israel, and North Korea), there are now about 15,000 intact nuclear weapons on the planet. Some of these weapons are deployed (about 5,000), and others are either stockpiled (about 4,500) or retired but intact. A massive use of these nuclear weapons would practically destroy the planet. But even a limited, and local, use would create unimaginable destruction, an enormous loss of lives, and ecological disaster.

The questions are:

1. Under what circumstances might these weapons be used?
2. Can other countries start building nuclear weapons, so increasing the dangers of nuclear use?

There are five circumstances where the risk of nuclear use is significant:

The first circumstance is nuclear use by mistake. Several weapons are always kept on permanent alert, in the case that there is enough information that an enemy nuclear attack is under way. Note that for intercontinental ballistic missiles, there is about 30 minutes between the notification/verification of an attack and the decision to launch. On September 26, 1983, a Russian colonel, Stanislav Petrov, made the decision to not abide by his duty and report a launch of five US missiles, deeming correctly

---

This talk was originally titled "The Risks of Nuclear War Today by Mistake, Miscalculation, Escalation . . ." —Editors.

that this was a false alarm, and thus avoiding a serious risk of nuclear war by mistake. On January 25, 1995, a Norwegian scientific rocket launched to observe the aurora borealis was mistakenly interpreted as an American nuclear missile. President Boris Yeltsin was handed the nuclear briefcase, but fortunately did not operate it. These are but two significant examples from a wide literature of similar "mistakes."

The second circumstance is nuclear use as a consequence of nuclear strategy. Planning for the possible use of nuclear weapons to countervail conventional inferiority increases the chance that a conventional conflict could be transformed into a nuclear one. This was typically a part of the nuclear strategy that NATO employed during the Cold War, and it is the strategy today in the case of Pakistan vis-à-vis India. In general, a no-first-use policy means that nuclear weapons would be used only after a verified nuclear attack—a policy that only China and India now have. Conversely, a policy of launch on warning (the launch of nuclear missiles only upon warning of an incoming nuclear attack) dramatically increases the probability of nuclear use by mistake. And both the US and Russia have a policy of launch on warning.

The third circumstance is inadvertent escalation. Independent of their existing nuclear strategies, a conflict involving states that possess nuclear weapons could inadvertently escalate into a nuclear conflict. For instance, the presence of so-called tactical nuclear weapons, and the need to disperse them in a time of crisis, could raise the dilemma of "use them or lose them." More generally, states possessing nuclear weapons, placed in a militarily critical situation, could decide to use (even a few) nuclear weapons to signal their resolve to not accept a possible defeat.

The fourth circumstance is "slipping out of control." The 1962 Cuban Missile Crisis was a typical example of a combination of misinformation, aggressive statements, and threats that could have resulted in a nuclear catastrophe. Later, in 1992, Fidel Castro told US secretary of defense Robert McNamara that Cuba had been willing to be destroyed, in a sort of national suicide, if the confrontation had "slipped out of hand." Good sense on both sides (in particular by Khrushchev), and a significant degree of good luck, avoided a catastrophe. Paradoxically, a somehow similar situation is now occurring in Northeast Asia. Can we count on the good sense of Kim Jong Un and President Trump? Let us hope so.

And the fifth circumstance includes terrorists, nonstate actors, and nuclear weapons. Nonstate actors can get their hands on nuclear weapons. In a state of relatively stable peace, this is difficult, given that nuclear weapons are kept in general under strict control. But in a situation of tension or conventional conflict, when nuclear weapons may be dispersed over the territory as a precautionary measure, nonstate actors could more easily get their hands on nuclear weapons. More significantly, nonstate actors could trigger a nuclear war between nuclear weapon states. For example, nonstate actors based in Pakistan could plan a significant terrorist attack on India, which, thinking incorrectly that Pakistan itself had organized such an attack, could decide to seize part of Pakistani territory (consistent with its so-called Cold Start strategy). And Pakistan has a policy of reacting with "tactical" nuclear weapons to a significant conventional attack. So a nonstate actor group can hope to trigger a nuclear confrontation between two countries that, as in the Indo-Pakistan case, the group considers to be either anti-Islamic or Islamic only by name and not "in reality."

In any case, by defining the risks of nuclear use, what is relevant is not just the number of existing nuclear weapons but also the number of states that possess them. So proliferation of nuclear weapons increases the risk of nuclear use.

The Nuclear Non-Proliferation Treaty (NPT) forbids the proliferation of nuclear weapons. It defines the five recognized nuclear weapon states—the United States, Russia, the United Kingdom, France, and China. Every other state member of the NPT is forbidden to acquire nuclear weapons. There are four significant states—Israel, India, Pakistan, and North Korea—that have nuclear weapons but are not members of the NPT. Apart from South Sudan, all other states are members of the NPT. But states that are members of the NPT can withdraw from the treaty (as North Korea did) with relatively few hassles.

A state can choose to acquire nuclear weapons to gain the prestige associated with their possession, for concerns about its own security, or both. The prestige associated with the possession of nuclear weapons is obviously very odd, but also unfortunately real, because the NPT-recognized nuclear weapon states are also permanent members of the UN Security Council (and the two states possessing the largest number of nuclear weapons are still referred to as superpowers). But the nuclear states, despite Article 6 of the NPT, are not proceeding resolutely to nuclear disarmament.

Security concerns obviously abound—for instance, throughout the Middle East—but only one state there, Israel, for now possesses nuclear weapons. But for how long will this be the situation? The Iranian civilian nuclear program has been effectively regulated by the Iran nuclear agreement, which is nevertheless now under stress as a result of the US questioning its validity. If the Iran nuclear agreement were to be dismantled, then there would be incentives for Iran to come back to the uncontrolled nuclear program that existed before the agreement. And Saudi Arabia and other states in the region will be watching carefully what Iran will do.

The situation of tension in Northeast Asia, and the ensuing nuclear risks for South Korea and Japan, may well push these two countries to consider the possibility of a nuclear option; they both have very well-developed civilian nuclear programs.

This brings us to the issue of the relation between civilian and military nuclear programs. Any country with a good civilian nuclear program can shift to a military nuclear program with relative ease. The barriers between civilian and military nuclear programs are related not so much to technological issues but to the control that is made over the civilian nuclear programs, mainly by the International Atomic Energy Agency in Vienna. States can agree to different types of control. The term "additional protocol" is used to define a particularly stringent and efficient control of civilian nuclear activities. In particular, a refusal to accept this additional protocol lowers the effectiveness of the control. There are states that, as a matter of principle, refuse to accept the additional protocol by claiming that they are not ready to accept any further discrimination beyond the distinction, encoded in the NPT, between nuclear weapon states and non–nuclear weapon states.

Finally, we must point out that some non–nuclear weapon states are protected by nuclear weapon states. This is the case for the NATO countries. Some of these states, while being non–nuclear weapon states according to the NPT, nevertheless host nuclear weapons, such as Italy, Germany, Belgium, the Netherlands, and Turkey. Other states could at some point also desire to be protected under such a "nuclear umbrella," and possibly host nuclear weapons belonging to other countries. And as this is arguably allowed under the NPT, then one can imagine a way of promoting the spread of nuclear weapons without contradicting the NPT.

A resolute action to completely eliminate nuclear weapons and ban them, just as chemical and biological weapons are banned, would not only be most desirable but would also remove the nuclear danger. The recent Nuclear Ban Treaty is an important step in the right direction, but many countries, and not only those possessing nuclear weapons, are not ready to sign it. It will be a long battle to promote this treaty and convince states to sign it. But it is a battle worth fighting.

20

Dealing with Weapons of Mass Destruction in the Middle East

Emily Landau

Normally, I am invited to speak at different conferences and seminars in order to share my findings and analysis with regard to my topics of research. But this is the first time I have been asked to give "testimony"—a term normally associated either with a religious setting or a court of law. I was thinking about how the term relates to my role here, and what resonated with me is the fact that in a court of law, a testimony is defined as a "solemn declaration usually made by a witness under oath." What I take from that definition is that this should be a well-thought-out and serious statement, one to which I am fully committed. So I have approached this undertaking with the utmost seriousness, in order to convey to you a clear message on this important topic.

My brief discussion of weapons of mass destruction (WMD) in the Middle East draws very much on the "paths to peace" that are mentioned in the title of this session, because paths to peace are determined by states and their policies, *not* the weapons in their possession. And indeed, at the end of the day, it is the states, not their weapons, that are the key to peaceful relations. Moreover, the regulation of WMD will not be fully effective if state interests and behavior are only assumed but not seriously addressed, especially with regard to the nature of states' relations and relationships with other states.

As for the humanitarian consequences of nuclear weapons use, these are obviously tremendously significant and indeed terrifying. However, over seven decades have passed since the first and only use of nuclear weapons at Hiroshima and Nagasaki, and over the course of those decades, nuclear weapons have come to be regarded as weapons of *deterrence* and *nonuse*.

Important international norms developed over the years that underscored the dangerous and destabilizing effect of nuclear proliferation; and the Nuclear Non-Proliferation Treaty (NPT) helped drive home that message, while also helping to keep the number of new nuclear states very low.

In fact—and I say this in light of the new efforts to ban the bomb—realistically speaking, the major challenge that the international community faces today in the nuclear realm comes *not* from the established nuclear states but rather from those states that have developed nuclear weapons programs in the last two and a half decades, in defiance of the nonproliferation norm, and indeed in violation of their own membership in the NPT.

When we consider the established nuclear states, we find that they have gradually carved out rules of the game in the nuclear realm—unspoken rules that have ensured a measure of strategic stability despite the great risks associated with nuclear weapons. In contrast, the new proliferators have breached the firm commitment they made not to develop nuclear weapons. As such, they are guilty of deceit with regard to their international commitment. Worse still, most have displayed aggressive regional and global behavior toward other states—behavior that raises serious doubts regarding their motivation for going nuclear, and whether they will adhere to the norm of nonuse. North Korea and Iran are the major states of concern in this regard today, and the threats emanating from North Korea over the past months have raised the specter of actual use of nuclear weapons, after seventy-two years.

When turning to the Middle East in particular, in order to more effectively deal with WMD, we must take a hard look at what is going on in the region—the poor relations, hate, terror, and open conflicts that cut in all directions.

We must also assess how nuclear and other WMD have played out for different states in the regional framework. What this means is that WMD must be assessed in context—*who* holds these weapons, and for *what purpose*. For Israel, it is assumed that nuclear deterrence has played the hugely significant role of helping to ensure survival in the face of existential threats.

But these weapons in the hands of irresponsible states can also be abused to wreak havoc—to kill indiscriminately, and to advance a state's aggressive regional hegemonic aims. The dangers associated with nuclear capabilities are very much a function of *whose hands they are in*, and how these states intend to integrate them in their strategic policy.

There is no doubt that the ultimate goal should be to rid the Middle East of WMD, but in striving for this goal, arms control advocates must understand that context *matters*. State policies and state behavior over time *matter*. Norms and rules of the game that regulate state behavior also *matter*. We will never get WMD arms control right if we buy into the fallacy that when discussing nuclear issues, it does not matter what state or states we are dealing with—that all differences among states are somehow erased or rendered irrelevant in the face of these dangerous weapons. Because the differences are *not* irrelevant—states are not identical, and the differences among them matter very much.

Just as France and North Korea are both nuclear states, but there are vast differences between them—and the same can be said for Britain and Pakistan, and for China and the United States, and I could go on—so there are differences among states in the Middle East: regarding their motivations, regional behavior, relationships with other states, and attitudes toward international commitments.

How should we confront the spread and use of WMD in the Middle East? By carving out arrangements that take context seriously—that address who the state is, what it has done in the WMD realm, and what it is striving to achieve through WMD possession. International commitments must be strictly upheld. Deceitful and dangerous violations by states cannot be tolerated, especially when these states threaten others, or kill their own population, such as seen recently in the chemical realm in Syria. But though international treaties are important for establishing norms against WMD possession and proliferation, the treaties themselves do not have effective means to take care of the violators—these must be dealt with by strong international actors that have the responsibility to uphold the treaties.

Ultimately, the goal is to work toward peaceful relations among states in the Middle East. When there is true peace, WMD will surely be unnecessary. And this brings me full circle to my opening remarks, namely, that the path to peace depends on states and their intentions.

In parallel, we should be striving to establish a regional framework that would enable discussion of WMD among the different players in the Middle East. But such a framework should not be geared to addressing WMD alone. Rather, it should include attention to state interests and relationships, and an entire range of regional security concerns. The goal should be to identify and try to build on common interests—even if only in a very limited way, initially, all with the aim of creating a safer and more secure Middle East for all.

21

Nuclear Proliferation in the Middle East: Resolving the Deadlock

Ayman Khalil

I start by conveying to you some good news and some bad news. On the positive side, we have a new treaty aiming at banning nuclear weapons. On the positive side also, we still have the Joint Comprehensive Plan of Action; in other words, the agreement with Iran is still intact and in one piece, so far. Yet, despite these positive reported developments, the bad news is that the Middle East is far from achieving or establishing its own nuclear-weapon-free zone.

Along the lines of this conference and the main themes of this conference, and to promote a nuclear-weapon-free world, I have to say that this is a huge undertaking that necessarily has to be achieved via incremental steps. One important and significant step needed to achieve this objective would be via—and only via—the establishment of a nuclear-weapon-free zone in the Middle East.

I hope you agree with me that the Middle East carries specific importance. Let me mention a few examples to illustrate this. Take, for instance, the Nuclear Non-Proliferation Treaty (NPT) regime, and more specifically the review mechanism that it entails. Of course, traditionally and historically the success or failure of the review conference has been strictly tied to the situation in the Middle East. An NPT review conference is considered a success if and only if it adequately deals with the situation in the Middle East. Hence the 2015 review conference was considered a failure, after the refusal of the United States, the United Kingdom, and Canada to join a consensus statement that supported a Middle East nuclear-weapon-free zone opposed by Israel, and the same applies to the 2005 review conference.

Speaking of the NPT, which is currently the only binding regime banning the proliferation of nuclear weapons, we have to say that this treaty suffers from a number of setbacks and gaps. The treaty provides a very good example that we are still living in a World War II environment. The nuclear weapon states happen to be the five permanent members of the United Nations Security Council. And of course, the nuclear weapon states also happen to be the victorious nations of World War II.

In fact, the nuclear nonproliferation regime has been exclusively drafted to reflect this specificity. For the first time ever, we have a treaty that is drafted to legitimize the possession of nuclear weapons only to victorious World War II nations.

For the first time, for the first time ever, we have a treaty—the NPT—that defines nuclear weapon states by date and not by merits, something that is unprecedented in other treaties. And within this context, I would like to congratulate the Vatican, the Holy See, for its pioneering, leading role and commitment to promote a legally binding comprehensive instrument to ban nuclear weapons that takes into consideration the loopholes and setbacks bypassed by the NPT.

I would like to shed more light on the Middle East. And of course, as you know, this is an important geographical area—the Cradle of Civilization, as it is called—and a major contributor to global problems and troubles. The Middle East is currently confronted with two challenges, two nuclear programs that are intended for different purposes and that have two different perceptions. The first is the Iranian nuclear program, which is becoming part of the national identity and pride in Iran, a program that is perceived by Iranians as a means to demand political leverage and to gain a foothold in the international arena. Meanwhile, the Israeli nuclear program is linked somehow to the existence and survival of Israel. This Israeli nuclear program has managed to manufacture tens if not hundreds of nuclear bombs and warheads sufficient to demolish an entire continent. I am personally shocked to hear my Israeli friends and colleagues say that they can sleep better at night knowing that they have a nuclear weapon.

And please forgive me for making a repeated reference to Israel, but I think this repeated reference is very important, and please understand that it is done because there is a deep and growing belief and conviction that the existence of an Iranian nuclear program was highly linked, motivated, and incentivized by the existence of an Israeli nuclear program.

I focus what is left of this presentation on providing four ideas that would promote and advance the creation of a nuclear-weapon-free zone in the Middle East. And I take this opportunity to invite the Holy See to adopt any of these ideas or any sets of these ideas, from this proposal.

First, we need to admit that the nuclear deterrence policy in Israel has not achieved its objectives in the Middle East. Let us face it, the existence of the Israeli nuclear arsenal did not prevent Saddam Hussein from launching his attacks, did not prevent Hezbollah from launching its attacks, and did not stop the Egyptians from regaining Sinai. Now, honestly speaking, I think the presence of highly sophisticated nonconventional capabilities to deter ill-equipped armies with modest conventional capabilities does not work out. It is not a match. So I think efforts should be shifted from developing mutually assured destruction ideologies—Mohamed ElBaradei mentioned that this is mad, and it is mad—into mutually assured survival ideologies. In a relatively small region such as the Middle East, we need to come to the joint conclusion that we should survive together.

Second, with the absence of tangible results within the peace process, in fact with a peace process that is in a coma at the moment, I think there is room for developing intermediate measures that could improve the situation, a set of technical confidence-building measures that can be introduced, such as the introduction of nonintrusive monitoring activities, whether environmental sampling, joint verification measures, or even "site"-seeing to particular facilities. I think this would have tangible results and a very important outcome. Another option is basically to collaborate in launching a regional network for detecting airborne nuclear contamination, which is highly needed and becoming a great necessity in the region.

Third, conditions for having all states in the region abiding by the NPT may not materialize in the short term. I mean, we have to be honest, the probability of Israel joining the NPT is very slim. And careful consideration of international models reveals that membership in the NPT should not be a precondition for joining the zone. So in principle, legally speaking, and from an international relations perspective, both sides, Arabs and Israel, could engage in good faith discussions to establish a zone.

Fourth, a number of other interesting options could also be taken into consideration, including the introduction of a protocol banning nonconventional launches, an extended version of a no-first-use treaty, and many others. Again, of course, these measures are highly needed in our part of the world.

PART VI

More Religious Voices

22

We Must Do No Less

Monsignor Robert W. McElroy

The Church proclaims that the promotion of peace is an integral element of Christ's ministry of redemption in the life of the world. Thus, any engagement of the Church in the central issues of nuclear arms that confront us in the current age must ultimately proceed from a commitment to conversion and grace that is equally rooted in the reality of the human condition, the substantive notion of peace that Christ holds out to us, and the dignity and solidarity that all of us share as children of the one God.

Such a search for redemptive action in the world must fully recognize the complex and daunting realities of international conflict, the power and prevalence of nuclear weapons, and the fundamental layers of inequality and historical oppression that underlie the seething animosities that infect the hearts of men and women. But the work of the Church can never be rooted principally in these realities, any more than the redemptive ministry of Christ himself was rooted in the sinfulness and failing of the human family. The ministry of the Church in the promotion of peace must at its core be one of conversion to new ways of thinking in the hearts of individuals and the international system.

In approaching the issues posed by nuclear weapons in the present moment, the Church must foster three dimensions of conversion in the world: a conversion from the prison of isolated national interests to the perspective of an integrated international common good; a conversion from the illusion of safety in nuclear strength to the reality of nuclear instability and proliferation; and a conversion from the reliance on weapons of war to the construction of weapons of peace. Each of these three conversions must be for the Church both an internal challenge and an external witness.

A Conversion to the International Common Good

We have just returned from a deeply spiritual moment of remembrance and prayer centered on the enormous contributions that Pope Saint John XXIII made to the life of the Church and the world. His monumental encyclical *Pacem in terris* was a resonating appeal to the conscience of the world to confront the very question with which we struggle in these days: the specter of nuclear war. But even more fundamentally, *Pacem in terris* was a profound call to the international community to recognize the imperatives of a truly universal, or international, common good that had emerged in the twentieth century, and to integrate this international common good with the specific common good of each nation. It is this embrace of the international common good that is the first level of conversion the Church must foster among citizens and nations in order to forge a sustainable solution to the nuclear dilemma.

The starting point for identifying the content of the international common good lies in the pivotal affirmations that God is the Father of the entire human family, that creation is a gift to every woman and man, that social structures must advance justice for all peoples, and that war is a massive failure of the entire human family. The centrality of the international common good in the modern era comes from understanding that many of the most profound human dilemmas that touch upon these affirmations of faith and humanity lie far beyond the ability of any nation or small group of nations to address justly in a globalized society.

The problem of nuclear weapons today is to a great degree a result of limited perspectives of national interests, which over the past fifty years have destroyed the original trajectory of the arms control regime that sought to make universal nuclear disarmament feasible. In short, the current nuclear crisis reflects the failure of nations to embrace an ethic of the universal common good in the very issue area where such an ethic was most cogent and most necessary.

Our conversion to the universal common good requires the recognition that the future of our world depends upon the willingness of all nations—especially the most powerful—to view their own national common good as interwoven in a mutually reinforcing pattern oriented toward the good of humanity as a whole.

Pope Francis spoke to this reality in his message to the 2014 Vienna Conference on the Humanitarian Impact of Nuclear Weapons: "Nuclear weapons are a global problem affecting all nations and impacting future generations and the planet that is our home. A global ethic is needed if we are to reduce the nuclear threat and work towards nuclear disarmament. Now, more than ever, technological, social and political interdependence urgently calls for an ethic of solidarity in the spirit of Pope John Paul II, which encourages people to work together for a more secure world, and a future that is increasingly rooted in moral values and responsibility on a global scale."

The Chilling Reality of Nuclear Arsenals

If the conversion to an ethic of the universal common good is the first foundation for progress in addressing the specter of nuclear arms, revealing clearly the chilling reality of the nuclear threat in the present moment is the second foundation. The Church must promote a conversion from the illusion that safety lies in the possession of nuclear weapons to the recognition that nuclear weapons constitute an increasingly destabilizing threat to humanity. The Church's fundamental goal in this transformation is to dispel the complacency that currently subverts and paralyzes international efforts at nuclear arms reductions, a complacency based upon denial and the false assumption that the logic of nuclear deterrence and proliferation has not fundamentally changed in the past fifty years.

The Holy See's intervention at the 2014 United Nations Disarmament Conference powerfully unmasked the illusory nature of the current nuclear regime: "Rather than providing security, as the defenders of nuclear deterrence contend, reliance on the strategy of nuclear deterrence has created a less secure world. In a multipolar world, the concept of nuclear deterrence works less as a stabilizing force and more as an incentive for countries to break out of the nonproliferation regime and develop nuclear arsenals of their own."

Taken together, the changes in the nuclear world order that have followed the end of the Cold War have systematically destroyed the foundations for an enduring ethic of deterrence. The resistance of the dominant nuclear powers to further substantial reductions in their nuclear arsenals has signaled to the community of nations that the commitment to end nuclear weapons in the world has been effectively abandoned. The toleration of newly emerging nuclear powers, sometimes for geopolitical reasons, betrays the commitment to stop proliferation and constitutes a double standard that undermines unity and progress. Major nuclear threats lie in the action of regional powers, and even more chillingly in the actions of terrorists and insurgents with aspirations for global violence.

The Church's role in witnessing to the peril that lies in the current course of nuclear proliferation can be a critical antidote to nationalist and militarist assertions that security and peace in any meaningful sense can be obtained through the possession of nuclear weapons. But for this witness to be effective, it must reach deeply into the Catholic community at its roots, and speak with particular prophetic power and certitude to the great nuclear powers that are on the cusp of modernization programs that will dramatically intensify the trajectory toward proliferation, and ultimately confrontation.

A Conversion from the Logic of War to the Logic of Peace

The final avenue through which the Church can contribute to the solution of the nuclear dilemma in the present moment is by propelling the conversion from the logic of war to the logic of peace. As followers of Jesus Christ, we are caught in powerful crosscurrents whenever we approach questions of war and peace. We recognize that on the most fundamental level, any recourse to war is incompatible with the Gospel of the Lord who taught us to see in every man and women our sister or brother in Christ. Yet we also know that evil exists in the world, both in the hearts of people and in the structures that human sin has created, and that at times evil cannot be opposed effectively without recourse to violence.

The Church is in the midst of a fundamental reappraisal of how to balance the Christian obligation to nonviolence with the need to resist evil in the world. The traditional norms of just war, particularly in the *ius ad bellum*, increasingly appear to be incapable of effectively constraining violence in the modern world. The power of nonviolence, which once was relegated to the category of romantic idealism, has emerged as a potent force for social transformation and building a lasting peace.

The Church must be a voice in the world constantly pointing humanity toward the path of nonviolence and the logic of peace. Too often, we acquiesce in the tolerance of weapons, threats, and war, concluding that the logic of war can at least hold evil at bay. But ultimately, it is the logic of war that, once unleashed, invites evil into the core of our world, our nation, and our hearts.

As Pope Francis underscored in his 2017 World Day of Peace Message, true discipleship in Jesus Christ at the present moment includes embracing his teaching about nonviolence: "Jesus himself lived in violent times. Yet he taught that the true battlefield, where violence and peace meet, is the human heart, for 'it is from within, from the human heart, that evil intentions come.' . . . Christ's message in this regard offers a radically positive approach."

This radically positive approach demands that we change the default position in our reasoning about war from acquiescence to the patterns and structures of violence to an active and persistent engagement with strategies of peace. Part of this engagement must be a radical dedication by the Church to bring the poor and the marginalized into the very heart of the international debate on war and peace. For it is the poor and the marginalized who suffer most greatly from the theft that the arms trade constitutes; it is they who endure the greatest cruelty in the midst of war; and it is they, because of their radical dependence, who may have a unique capacity to convey to us who live in comfort that on the issue of nuclear weapons, we all stand in radical dependence and vulnerability.

In 2008 Pope Benedict, surveying the nuclear landscape in the world, lamented that an ethic of complacency and even a toleration of limited nuclear expansion had become inextricably intertwined with the ethic of deterrence, and that as a result the possession of nuclear weapons was increasingly becoming a sign of great power status, a temptation for newly emerging powers to defend their interests, and a spur to modernization.

"In difficult times such as these," Pope Benedict wrote, "it is truly necessary for all persons of goodwill to come together to reach concrete agreements aimed at an effective demilitarization, especially in the area of nuclear arms. At a time when the process of nuclear non-proliferation is at a standstill, I feel bound to entreat those in authority to resume with greater determination negotiations for a progressive and mutually agreed dismantling of existing nuclear weapons. In renewing this appeal, I know that I am echoing the desire of all those concerned for the future of humanity."

For the Church to contribute meaningfully to the attainment of such a dismantling, it must help both the Catholic community and the nations of the world to engage in new forms of thinking: a conversion to an ethic of the universal common good, a conversion to the chilling reality that nuclear arsenals undermine rather than secure peace, and a conversion to building strategies of peace in recognition that the strategies of war are bankrupt and destructive. *Pacem in terris* was monumentally important because it called the world to new ways of thinking. The Church at this pivotal moment must do no less.

23

Transforming the Human Spirit

Hiromasa Ikeda

On July 7, 2017, the Treaty on the Prohibition of Nuclear Weapons (TPNW) was adopted by the United Nations negotiating conference. This was a historic and concrete step toward the abolition of nuclear weapons. As a civil society organization, the Soka Gakkai International (SGI) maintained a deep interest and active involvement in the negotiating process.

It was John F. Kennedy who said, "Our problems are manmade—therefore, they can be solved by man. And man can be as big as he wants. No problem of human destiny is beyond human beings. Man's reason and spirit have often solved the seemingly unsolvable—and we believe they can do it again."

This way of thinking strongly resonates with that of the SGI. The question then becomes how best to take on the challenges that face us. The SGI's activities for peace, in particular for the abolition of nuclear weapons, arise from the philosophical stance that a transformation in the spirit of one person can transform society. This idea has been expressed by SGI president Daisaku Ikeda: "A great human revolution in just a single individual will help achieve a change in the destiny of a nation, and, further, will enable a change in the destiny of all humankind."

We can anticipate two objections to this approach. The first is that if the only way to achieve nuclear disarmament is by transforming the human spirit, then a world without nuclear weapons is an impossibility. Nuclear disarmament is already extremely difficult; if transforming the human spirit is then added as a necessary precondition, the goal of a world free from nuclear weapons becomes unreachable. A second objection might be to question whether it is in fact possible to transform the human spirit. This touches on the core questions of human existence.

To respond first to the second objection, we believe that the spiritual life of humans is characterized by its diversity and mutability. Neither good nor evil are fixed realities intrinsic to human life, but are always subject to the possibility of change. We manifest different aspects of our inner life through our proactive engagements with others and in response to the ways they act on us. Crucially, we believe that sublime possibilities of wisdom, compassion, and courage exist as potentialities inherent in all human life. Our practice as Buddhists lies in the ceaseless effort to bring forth those best potentialities in both ourselves and others. What we term "transforming the human spirit" means making manifest the best qualities already inherent in human life.

Then to respond to the first objection, I note that we consider difficult challenges such as nuclear disarmament to be prime opportunities to bring forth the more positive aspects of the human spirit. To engage the challenge of abolishing nuclear weapons is to confront the most demonically destructive aspects of human life that underlie nuclear weapons and their radical negation of the dignity and sanctity of life. Buddhism describes these destructive impulses as the "three poisons" of anger, greed, and the fundamental ignorance or folly from which they arise. We do not, therefore, view transforming the human spirit as a necessary condition for the achievement of nuclear disarmament. Rather, we believe that by taking on this immensely difficult challenge, each of us can develop the best qualities inherent in the human spirit. This is our core approach.

It goes without saying that this is not easy. It is vital that in confronting these issues we continue to foster new awareness and new sustaining motivation. Education can and must play a crucial role in this regard. And it is for this reason that education—providing learning opportunities—has been a consistent feature of our activities.

Today, continued possession of nuclear weapons is justified for reasons of national security, on the basis of nuclear deterrence theory. How, then, do we help people awaken from the mad nightmare of such deterrence, by which the world's citizens are held hostage and "peace" is maintained by a balance of terror? This is the key question.

To do this requires that those engaged in the movement for nuclear disarmament put forward a new vision of security, one that is easily understood, robust, and appealing. We need to awaken people from the present nightmare with the bright lights of a new vision. Concepts such as integral disarmament, human security, and human development all indicate the orientation for such a vision.

Within the disarmament field, humanitarian concerns have provided such and orientation. They have helped introduce a human perspective to the security discourse. The humanitarian discourse has led to an explicit recognition within the international community of the impermissible nature of nuclear weapons, contributing importantly to the realization of the TPNW.

Underlying the humanitarian discourse has been the assertion that the nuclear weapons issue is not just a question of international law but also has a distinctly ethical and moral dimension. Here the role played by the world's religious traditions has been noteworthy. His Holiness Pope Francis issued a statement to both the 2014 Vienna Conference and the TPNW negotiating conference held in New York this year, positively affecting the debate. For its part, the SGI actively participated in the initiative by Faith Communities Concerned about Nuclear Weapons—which issued a total of eight joint statements to the UN General Assembly, the review conference for the Nuclear Non-Proliferation Treaty, and the TPNW negotiating conference—urging the prohibition and elimination of nuclear weapons.

The preamble to the TPNW recognizes the efforts made by religious leaders. This is a clear acknowledgment that the voices raising ethical or moral concerns have been an indispensable element in the international discourse over the years.

Within the SGI, we have given sustained consideration to the kind of approach that would most effectively engage a broad-based public constituency in the debate on nuclear weapons abolition. The concept we developed is expressed in the phrase, "Everything you treasure." The desire to protect the people and things we love is a core human sentiment. Propelled by this, we humans have built homes, woven fabric, and raised crops and harvested them. At the same time, the urge to protect what we value—the people we love—has propelled the development of military technologies. The destructive power of weapons continued to grow over the course of centuries, culminating in 1945 in the development and use of nuclear weapons. As Albert Einstein put it, "The release of atom power has changed everything except our way of thinking."[1] Indeed, despite the fact that we today live lives that are profoundly interdependent, how consciously aware of this reality are we?

If an awareness of our deep interdependence could truly take hold in the minds of each individual, we would become conscious of the fact that any harm done to others will in some form redound to us. This is the foundation for the ethos that SGI president Ikeda has expressed as the commitment not to build one's happiness on the suffering of others. It is for this reason that our movement has focused on expanding the reach of empathy. This starts by encouraging frank dialogue among people based on the universal human desire to protect the things we treasure. This can in turn foster a shared awareness that nuclear weapons—in any hands—are dangerous and wrong as a means of protecting the things and people we treasure. On this basis, we can pursue the elimination of nuclear weapons as the shared global undertaking of humankind.

This was the thinking behind the launch of our campaign People's Decade for Nuclear Abolition, in 2007, and for our collaboration with the International Campaign to Abolish Nuclear Weapons (ICAN), recipients of the 2017 Nobel Peace Prize, in promoting global grassroots efforts in awareness-raising. The exhibition we developed in cooperation with ICAN, titled "Everything You Treasure—For a World Free from Nuclear Weapons," has to date been held in eighty cities in nineteen countries, attracting numerous visitors.

The challenge of initiating dialogue is something that can be taken up by anyone. Dialogue holds limitless possibilities. What starts as a simple conversation on a given topic can naturally deepen into richer forms of dialogue over time. The core of the SGI's religious activities is the local small group discussion meeting which brings together people from different social backgrounds where they exchange and share their experiences in faith. We believe that this kind of dialogic platform can be adapted and applied to the movement to abolish nuclear weapons. The various exhibitions that the SGI has developed over the years are based on this same formula, in that we seek to generate forums for dialogue. The exhibitions have become the site of spontaneous dialogue among viewers, generating a sense of empathetic connection and shared concern. This in turn can give rise to action and solidarity and even a new generation of citizen leaders. We further believe that this kind of dialogic approach can be applied to all forms of diplomatic effort toward the realization of a world without nuclear weapons.

As another of the SGI's activities, we have supported efforts by young people to record war experiences, in particular those of the Hibakusha. This of course provides an opportunity for youth to learn about the realities of war and nuclear weapons. But even more, it is through such encounters and dialogue that young people can develop and grow as leaders. Through such activities, we have sought to involve a broad spectrum of participation and to develop youth leadership.

As I have sought to summarize, the SGI's movement for nuclear weapons abolition focuses on the inner diversity and mutability of human life. Through dialogue, we seek to extend the reach of empathy and raise popular awareness. These I believe are the special characteristics of our efforts, which may be understood as a grassroots program of peace and disarmament education. The role of peace and disarmament education is referenced in the preamble to the TPNW. Article 12 calls for efforts to universalize the treaty. In light of the origins of the treaty, which was drafted with the participation and contributions of civil society, it is clear that civil society can make important and indispensable contributions here also.

Nuclear weapons are dangerous from a security perspective. From an ethical and moral perspective, they are wrong. This renders them unacceptable in any hands. Today, with the geopolitical risks of nuclear conflict at almost unprecedented levels, it is vital that this awareness be shared widely by all people.

We are determined to continue to collaborate with the diverse actors that share the SGI's goal of encouraging this awareness through peace and disarmament education.

Note

1. Cf. "Atomic Education Urged by Einstein," *New York Times*, May 25, 1946: "The unleashed power of the atom has changed everything save our modes of thinking and we thus drift toward unparalleled catastrophe."

24

Migrations and Wars

Monica Attias

War and refugees have always been present in human history. But in the twenty-first century, displacement caused by war has become a massive phenomenon, a typical expression of globalization. The language of international politics is increasingly bellicist, in words and deeds.

As a result of war, forced displacement has seen an acceleration in recent years, reaching unprecedented levels. According to data from the Office of the UN High Commissioner for Refugees, in our world there are 65.6 million individuals, half of whom are under eighteen, who are forcibly displaced because of conflict, violence, and persecution. A total of 75,000 are unaccompanied minors or children separated from their families. This means, in practical terms, that about 28,000 people a day must leave their homes to seek refuge.

Their stories often remain buried in the Mediterranean, in the desert, and at the frontiers where they are rejected. They remain hidden in the refugee camps where asylum seekers are waiting not only for a better future but simply for a future. No country can face this situation by itself. And international challenges cannot be solved by raising walls.

Faced with media images of children and families who lose their lives while they search for a safe haven, there is a wide sense of bewilderment and powerlessness. After the visit of the Holy Father to Lampedusa and the shipwreck of October 3, 2013, where 368 people lost their lives, the Community of Sant'Egidio began to think about what could be done to avoid these tragedies.

I would like to share how the idea of Humanitarian Corridors came into being. The Humanitarian Corridors are the implementation of safe and legal passages for the most vulnerable victims of war and conflict. The initiative was launched at the end of 2015 by the Community of Sant'Egidio, together with the Waldensian and Methodist churches and the Federation of Evangelical Churches in Italy, under a protocol signed with the Foreign and Home Affairs Ministries in Italy, to bring Syrian refugees displaced in Lebanon. In 2017—in partnership with the Italian Catholic Bishops' Conference, Caritas Italy, and the Migrantes Foundation—a new corridor from Ethiopia for Eritreans and Somalis and South Sudanese was established. Before the end of 2017, they welcomed the first group of refugees from the Horn of Africa.

The value of this initiative is first and foremost that of being a Christian response to the tragedy of war, forced migration, and the collateral plague of human smuggling and trafficking. It is a response to the globalization of indifference. Moreover, it is an ecumenical response: an ecumenism of charity that goes beyond theological controversies and finds a concrete expression in a common effort to help the suffering.

Since February 2016 the Humanitarian Corridors project has flown about 1,000 people to Italy, and 1,500 more are expected; women, children, sick and elderly people, and victims of torture have taken a journey of hope on a regular airline and not on the boats of death. They have flown over the sea, not needing to put their lives at risk by sailing. A first group of refugees came through the same project in France, which expects the arrival of 500 people from Lebanon. A protocol was signed among Sant'Egidio, the Federation of the Protestant Churches of France, the French Catholic Bishops' Conference, Secours Catholique, and the French government.

This is a pilot project, the first of its kind in Europe. It is proposed as a replicable model in the Schengen area, implementing a virtuous synergy among churches, institutions, and civil society. That is why negotiations are under way with other countries, including Belgium and Andorra.

How is it possible to bring people legally? The basic principle is to grant people in "conditions of vulnerability," regardless of their religious or ethnic affiliation, legal entry into Italian territory with humanitarian visas and the possibility to later submit applications for asylum. This is a visa with limited territorial validity, pursuant to Article 25 of the European visa regulations, which provides for a member state the possibility of issuing visas on humanitarian grounds, because of national interest or international obligations. For France, instead, the legal instrument is a long-term visa provided for by national law.

A second important element is the security that the project guarantees to hosting countries. An identity check is carried out before the entry of refugees. The issuing of visas by the embassies in Lebanon and Ethiopia provides the necessary controls.

But I would say that the hospitality and integration of vulnerable refugees is the aspect that has most affected positively the life of the churches and of civil society. These are under the responsibility of the sponsoring organizations, and the initiative is totally self-funded. Once the refugees arrive, they are taken in charge by parishes, religious congregations, families, local communities, and people of goodwill. Instead of big refugee centers, they are hosted in apartments and family-like facilities.

Recently, some members of Sant'Egidio went for a tour in Italy, to visit the Syrian families hosted through the Humanitarian Corridors project. They were struck by the positive attitudes of the Italian hosts. Integration is actually easier than expected. Syrian boys and girls already speak Italian, less than a year after their arrival. Most of all, they witnessed the positive impact that the sponsorship of a family or a group of people has had on the local community, that is, on the Italians: "Now everybody gives a hand," said the mother of a family living in a small town. Activities such as accompanying people to receive health care, administrative clearances, job matching, shopping, and language teaching—in sum, the responsibilities deriving from an integration project—require the existence of a proactive Christian community, or a section of civil society.

Let me underline another aspect. The same woman explained how the sponsorship project uncovered the generosity and talent of the people: "It is not true that Christians are powerless. A broad and crosscutting network of helpers has been created, and the communities now benefit from new friendships and relationships." This is the sustainable legacy of the sponsorship operation, a legacy that is now mentioned in governmental documents as a best practice in dealing with refugee integration. We hope this legacy will represent a breakthrough in the culture of indifference.

Pope Francis mentioned the Humanitarian Corridors initiative during the Angelus on March 6, 2016, saying that it is a concrete commitment to peace and life, combining the values of solidarity and security. Sant'Egidio has supported the desire of the Holy Father to bring refugee families from Lesbos to Italy, as a sign for Christians that something can be done.

When Pope Francis later came to visit the Shrine of Contemporary Martyrs of the Christian Faith at the Roman Basilica of Saint Bartholomew, he recalled a conversation with a refugee man in Lesbos: "I found a thirty-year-old man with three children. He looked at me and said: 'Father, I am a Muslim. My wife was Christian. Terrorists came and asked us our religion. They saw she had a cross and told her to throw it away. She didn't, and they cut her throat in front of me. We loved one another so much!' This is the icon I bring today [to this Church] as a present."

25

The Social and Moral Responsibilities of Knowledge Workers

Drew Christiansen, SJ

I am honored to be invited to address this afternoon's session on the social and moral responsibilities of scientists. This conference on Perspectives for a World Free from Nuclear Weapons and for Integral Disarmament is a major step on the part of the Holy See in advancing its policy in favor of integral nuclear disarmament, after its signing and ratification of the new Treaty on the Prohibition of Nuclear Weapons this past September.

I have taken the liberty to reformulate the title of my talk to read "The Social and Moral Responsibilities of Knowledge Workers," because in American usage, the term "scientists" is usually taken in a restrictive sense to mean natural scientists: physicists, chemists, biologists, and the like. But, as Alessio Pecorario confirmed to me, the Italian usage, *scienziati*, like the German *wissenschafter*, is a broader category embracing learned professionals and scholars, and so also encompassing other disciplines related to nuclear weapons, including just war analysts and strategic theorists. Theorists of nuclear strategy, though not directly involved in the deterrent, nonetheless have serious responsibilities that need to be worked through. In the brief space available, however, I take a few short steps toward addressing the responsibilities of just war analysts as a template for expanded treatment of the larger topic in the near future.[1]

I imagine two immediate audiences for this endeavor: The first consists of knowledge workers themselves who, in light of the Church's contemporary teaching and diplomatic commitments to nuclear disarmament, are wondering what their responsibilities may be with regard to their work. Second, I am thinking of the pastors and pastoral workers—bishops, priests, pastoral counselors, and spiritual directors—who are being asked for guidance by workers in the nuclear weapons field.[2]

Growing toward a Consensus

The Church's teaching has evolved from a conditioned acceptance of nuclear deterrence in the 1980s to rejection of deterrence as an unacceptable moral rationalization for nuclear armament in the 2000s, to strong support for nuclear disarmament in recent years, leading to approval for the Ban Treaty just this year.[3] Thinking Catholics are right to ask, "What should I do?" And I would be less than candid if I did not report a degree of consternation among those serious about their Catholic faith that they have not received clearer guidance on how to address their civic and professional obligations with respect to nuclear weapons in light of the Church's current teaching condemning "the possession and threat to use nuclear weapons," the substance of deterrence.[4] For their part, at this point, when many bishops hesitate to give a blanket answer to this question, they are prudently exercising their pastoral office until they have greater clarity about the issues involved. This hesitation is not unprecedented, for in past generations popes, bishops, and councils often consulted theologians and canonists and waited for them to sort out issues before pronouncing or intervening in a controversy.[5]

To offer clearer moral advice, the Church's pastors need to build a consensus in the Church, wait for it to gather into a settled judgment on the part of moral theologians and bishops, and into a firm conviction in faith among the people of God. The response to the US bishops' multiyear, open process in drafting *The Challenge of Peace* during the first term of the Reagan administration (1981–85) demonstrates that not just ephemeral public opinion but also the more mature *public judgment* can move in the direction of Church teaching where there is wide and full engagement on the part of the faithful.[6]

The Oakland Paradigm

If we were to consider these issues merely in the abstract, there might be reason to think we stand at an impasse between the moral ideal and the pressing realities of a nuclear-armed world. But we have a historical precedent to which we can turn to see how scientists' options can change with the development of the Church's teaching—in this case, the options of physical scientists. After *The Challenge of Peace* appeared, Bishop John S. Cummins of Oakland sponsored a series of conferences to address the implications of the letter for scientists, both Catholics and others, working at the University of California's Lawrence Livermore Laboratories with theologians and ethicists from the Graduate Theological Union in Berkeley. Together, they probed the issues posed by the letter.

These deliberations resulted in new choices both for the scientists and their institutions. Some scientists, at least, moved from designing bombs to working on verification techniques. Aided by energy policies set in place earlier by the Carter administration, others along with their laboratories shifted the direction of their research from nuclear weaponry to alternative energy development. In the present US political climate, the paths to career and policy change may not be as easy. But the Oakland dialogues took place during the days of the Reagan administration, which were just as discouraging, and they offer a pastoral model for bishops and bishops' conferences to function as conveners of moral conversations and leaders of moral discernment for scientists and other learned professionals in the nuclear weapons business.

Adult Moral Formation

The Oakland dialogues also present a model for adult moral formation. Adults learn better in interactive settings where their own experience is engaged as they were in the Oakland Diocese dialogues. In addition, extensive public deliberation over the drafts of *The Challenge of Peace* led, in my judgment, to wider knowledge and acceptance of the bishops' teaching than it would have if the letter had been issued *de caelo* on the authority of the bishops alone without public engagement.[7] The pastoral letter's long-lasting moral authority in the United States, including among the US military, came in part because of the open, inviting, and trusting way in which the bishops of that day shaped the document they finally approved. There were hearings in various places, and the successive drafts of the pastoral were widely distributed in the media and debated by people both inside and outside the Church. As a result, various constituencies, even those who were initially opposed to or critical of the letter, eventually accepted its teaching employed in their courses and the professional training of their colleagues.

Communities of Moral Discourse and Discernment

The Oakland model also provides a way to think about collective moral discernment in the Church. The Second Vatican Council affirmed that the whole "Church has always had the duty of scrutinizing the signs of the time and interpreting them in light of the gospel."[8] Later, Pope Paul VI, and now Pope Francis, spoke about the responsibility of the whole Church, and communities within the Church, to discern the signs of the times.[9] Furthermore, given the diversity and complexity of today's world, both popes confessed the inability of the pope alone to read the signs of the times, and accordingly the need for diverse communities to undertake this discernment in communion with their bishops.[10] The Oakland meetings were not themselves explicitly exercises in communal discernment, though many scientists made such discernments on the basis of those convenings, but they were a model, at least, for the Church as "a community of moral discourse," a first step on the way to discernment.[11]

Maturation of Judgment

Finally, the discernment model taught by Pope Paul VI and Pope Francis allows for both the maturation of collective judgment on the part of the faithful and for its gradual permeation throughout the Church.[12] In this fashion, moral teaching may arise, in Cardinal Newman's words, as "a conspiracy of bishops and faithful."

Accordingly, the teaching will be more readily received as an authentic expression of the Church's faith.[13] As envisaged by the council and advanced by Pope Paul VI and Pope Francis, however, communal discernment assumes not passive but engaged and active communities of faith.

Recent Church Teaching

The first efforts of the Church's magisterium to articulate the responsibilities of scientists toward the nuclear deterrent were of a general sort. They provide us with direction but without specific guidelines or a method for prescribing the responsibilities of knowledge workers. The Cuban Missile Crisis prompted Pope Saint John XXIII to write *Pacem in terris*, but in those early years of Catholic emancipation from "the long nineteenth century," Pope John primarily focused on the need for lay people to be scientifically competent and to participate in public affairs.[14] He argued against allowing a two-culture mentality to split the life of faith from scientific and technical expertise, and urged instead "that human beings, in the unity of their own consciences, should so live and act . . . as to create a synthesis between scientific, technical and professional elements on the one hand, and spiritual values on the other."[15]

In its reflections on the destructive power of modern weapons, the Second Vatican Council simply urged government officials and military leaders to "give unremitting thought to the awesome responsibilities which is theirs before God and the human race."[16] The US bishops, noting the role of science in precipitating the problems of the nuclear age, in their 1983 pastoral letter, urged scientists' involvement in the solution of those problems. "Surely," the bishops wrote, "equivalent dedication of scientific minds to reverse current trends, and to pursue concepts as bold and adventuresome in favor of peace as those which in the past have magnified the risks of war, could result in dramatic benefits to all humanity."[17] Ten years later, in "The Harvest of Justice Is Sown in Peace," the bishops urged American Catholics to renew their collective "'No' to the idea of nuclear war."[18] But the US bishops offered no explicit moral guidance for those in the field of nuclear weapons research and strategic analysis.

Even a notable study by the moral theologians John Finnis, Germain Grisez, and Joseph Boyle, which attempted a detailed casuistry of the responsibilities of various actors in the nuclear arena, offered no advice to scientists, whether physical scientists or nuclear theorists. They did address the responsibilities of legislators, submarine commanders, and key-turners, but not those of bomb designers, builders, or strategists. For citizens in general, they argued for a positive obligation "to take such opportunities as their prior responsibilities permit to bear witness to their alienation from their nation's deterrence policy."[19]

So, allow me, then, to venture to address, in a preliminary fashion, the responsibilities of one broad class of scholars, namely, just war analysts (and especially the moral theologians among them), a company to which I myself belong, with respect to the Church's teaching on nuclear weapons policy and deterrence strategy.

A Preliminary Sketch of the Responsibilities of Just War Analysts

Specification of the responsibilities of just war analysts should be done with respect to their roles and relations and, where there are professional codes of conduct or legal regulations, the prescriptions of the rules governing their profession as well.[20] Relations are the fundamental category, and, for our limited purposes here, the most germane relations are those of the analysts to Church and civil society—the Church because it remains a primary agent, as Pope Francis has written, for "continuing efforts to limit the use of force by the application of moral norms"; and civil society because it constitutes the public square where we debate our fundamental values and explore how they should shape the institutions of our common life.[21] Now, following Pope Francis's condemnation of the threat to use and possession of nuclear weapons, let me propose a set of responsibilities for just war analysts with respect to nuclear deterrence.

Eight Responsibilities of Just War Analysts

Although Pope John XXIII had already identified abolition of nuclear weapons as the goal of Catholic Social Teaching, since the 1980s the operative principle had been "strictly conditioned moral acceptance" of nuclear weapons for the purpose of deterrence. But, by the 2000s, the Vatican began to critique deterrence as an obstacle to disarmament, and in 2017 Pope Francis finally condemned deterrence and declared the elimination as the goal of any moral nuclear weapons policy.

Positive Peace

With respect to nuclear abolition, the overall task, as my late colleague John Howard Yoder argued, is to make just war analysis "credible" by setting it in the broader Catholic peace tradition.[22] In this new moment, *the first responsibility for just war analysts, I would argue, is to assess nuclear weapons policy, and especially deterrence, within the larger context of an ethic of peace.* For Catholic just war thinkers, this would embrace not just the Church's developing teaching on nonviolence and just peace but also the fuller teaching on positive peace, including human rights, integral development, and care for creation.[23] Only when analysts integrate the full implications of human rights, integral development, and care for creation into their thinking on issues of war and peace will they be able to honestly—and, yes, competently—address the risks and the costs of armed conflict and nonviolent direct action.

There are two reasons for integrating the Catholic ethic of peace with our moral analyses of conflict. First, the practice of just war thinking tends to be carried out in a crisis mode, where the pressures of public debate induce a focus on blood and fire. Instead, just war thinkers need to take into account the growing body of knowledge and practice of peacemaking by both secular and religious actors.[24]

Furthermore, Augustine's identification of *peace as the substance of right intention* in warfare should not be allowed to vaporize into a mere formality. It needs to be fully updated in light of contemporary social science, international humanitarian law, moral philosophy, theology, and church teaching. Only when these judgments are informed by a fuller, more comprehensive understanding of the requirements of peace, including the demands of integral disarmament, may practical judgments about fulfillment of the norm be taken seriously.

Engaging the Different Schools of Thought

The very broad college of just war thinkers is fissured in two ways. First, there is the fault line between those I call permissive just war thinkers, who tend to approve of any military practice or policy, and others who, intent on preventing and limiting armed conflict, apply the tradition more stringently. The second fissure lies between just war thinkers, even the stringent ones, and those in the nonviolent and just peace traditions. The credibility of contemporary just war thinking would be greatly enhanced if, at a minimum, the practitioners would alert their audiences to where they stand in these debates. But, as a practical rule, I would argue that *the second responsibility of analysts of peace and war would be to seriously engage thinkers on all sides of the theoretical divides: permissive/stringent and just war / nonviolence approaches.* Engaging the permissive school is necessary to avoid and, if possible, to correct abuse of the just war tradition in rationalizing the extremes of armed conflict, an extraordinarily grave need in the case of nuclear weapons. Engaging the cutting edge of the nonviolence / just peace school is required to inform the analysis of war and peace issues with not only the best of current knowledge on the alternatives to armed force but also to establish what would count for success in a given conflict. There has been growing clarification of the latter in recent discussion of the *ius post bellum*, that is, norms of postwar justice.[25]

Maintaining the Firebreak

Furthermore, nuclear strategists speak of the firebreak between nuclear and conventional war. A recurrent problem with nuclear ethics is that when it is carried out repeatedly over time, it seems like just another exercise in the casuistry of war. Just as weapons designers attempt to make nuclear weapons more usable, so some nuclear ethicists try to identify peculiar circumstances in which it might just be permissible for the weapons to be used. That slide to normality must be resisted. In ethics, as in military strategy, the firewall must be maintained.

Just as John Paul II and the US bishops asked Christians and people of goodwill "to say 'No' to nuclear war," so today we must say "no" to the possession and development of nuclear weapons, as the UN Treaty to Prohibit Nuclear Weapons did this summer.[26] *The third responsibility of just war thinkers is to maintain the firebreak between the casuistry of conventional armed war and that of nuclear weapons policy.* They must treat nuclear war and nuclear weapons as a wholly different class of problems demanding an exceptional degree of caution in their analyses. We should cease to imagine nuclear weapons as tools for us to manage, but rather as a curse we must banish. We need to think about them, as the Second Vatican Council said of modern war, "with an entirely new attitude."[27]

Acknowledging the Shift in World Opinion

The *fourth responsibility* follows from the third: *Today's just war analysts, especially but not exclusively Catholics, have a responsibility to integrate into their scholarship the rejection of nuclear weapons by the Treaty to Prohibit Nuclear Weapons passed at the UN this summer.*[28] The treaty prohibits the development, testing production, manufacture, acquisition, possession or stockpiling of nuclear weapons or other nuclear explosive devices.[29] Analysts must take into account this shift in the law of nations, the *ius gentium*, as represented by the majority of the UN member states that authorized the conference negotiating the Ban Treaty, by the nations belonging to nuclear-free zones and the civil society organizations supporting nuclear abolition, and reject the further legitimation of defense strategies based on nuclear weapons, as supposed legacy rights of the permanent five members of the UN Security Council under the Nuclear Non-Proliferation Treaty.[30]

Making the Teaching "Church-Wide and Parish-Deep"

Making Church teaching on nonproliferation "church-wide and parish-deep" are the words of my colleague Gerald Schlabach, in the context of the challenge to Catholicism with respect to nonviolence.[31] I would adapt his maxim into a fifth responsibility for moral theologians wrestling with issues of peace and war: *Catholic moral theologians who are also just war analysts have the responsibility with respect to global moral problems, above all nuclear abolition, to make the Church's teaching "church-wide and parish-deep."* The Church needs their expertise to fill an enormous pastoral gap in the knowledge and practice of contemporary Catholic social teaching on this matter. The professoriate deserves its autonomy, but the alienation that sometimes afflicts relations between bishops and the academy needs to be overcome for the sake of the global common good. In this new moment, for the good of the Church and the future of the planet, the academic and episcopal magisteria must work together.[32]

A Forensic Process

Further, I would argue that just war analysis—or, more exactly, the moral analysis of issues of peace and war—is not a disengaged, neutral academic activity. Rather, it is a forensic exercise, a contribution to ecclesial and public debate, articulating pastoral and public policy as part of our common life. It operates within a social system that defines, applies, and enforces rules and policies related to the building of peace and the prevention and limitation of war. Its participants include not just philosophers, theologians and legal scholars, bishops, pastors, confessors, and pastoral counselors but also military lawyers, courts martial, military training systems, and conscientious objectors. Thus, *the sixth responsibility of analysts of issues of peace and war is to purposefully participate in and contribute to a public dialogue that establishes, adapts, applies, and enforces societal norms related to the building up of peace and the conduct of war.* Today, the forensic character of just war thinking requires their involvement in critiquing nuclear deterrence and pioneering paths toward a nonnuclear peace. As such, analysts share responsibility in a larger network of scholars and professionals who together build up the conditions of peace and defend it against the destructive effects of violent conflict and the temptations of a warrior mentality. It is out of that set of mutually defining interactions that sharper, more direct, and satisfying answers to nuclear scientists' doubts and honest questioning will emerge.

In the week after the conference, unique evidence of the practice of just war thinking as a forensic process was offered by two US Air Force generals, the current commander and a former commander of the Strategic Air Command, who testified that they would refuse illegal orders to fire nuclear weapons. Interestingly, both indicated that an illegal order was determined by a complex judgment applying just war norms, not by a literal reading of black-letter law.[33] General John Hyten, the current Strategic Air Command commander, included among the norms for judging an order illegal the recent norm of "unnecessary suffering." The recent US Senate hearings on the president's sole authority to launch nuclear weapons, to which retired general C. Robert Kehler gave testimony, also illustrated in a dramatic way the forensic character of just war thinking.[34]

In our day, moreover, public forums are the primary loci where public opinion can be built to resist policies of deterrence. As the US bishops wrote in *The Challenge of Peace*, "Especially in a democracy, public opinion can passively acquiesce to policies and strategies, or it can, through a series of measures, indicate the limits beyond which a government should not proceed."[35] Just as the US bishops in the 1980s encouraged "resistance" to nuclear war fighting, so today Catholics and people of goodwill need to assert their opposition to nuclear deterrence as a policy of defense. Fellow citizens, as the US bishops and others recognized, make up a primary audience for just war analysis. Although social media today will certainly have a role in building opposition to deterrence, the more considered methods of the past will still have a significant role in establishing public judgment with respect to deterrence by providing solid intellectual, political, and religious foundations for that public judgment. In processes of public education and deliberation, just war thinkers will undoubtedly play a role.

For centuries moral theologians, confessors, and spiritual directors played a role in conscience formation for policymakers, military leaders, and ministers involved in state policy.[36] Bishops can convene the faithful for moral conversation and discernment; they ought to expound Catholic social teaching and preach it, and they can discreetly exercise their disciplinary authority toward egregious public sinners.[37] The Second Vatican Council also urged that they address the great public issues of the day and proposed the formation of bishops' conferences, so they can collaborate for the common good.[38]

Just war thinkers, moral theologians, and philosophers can and should assist bishops in their work. They serve a tradition of moral wisdom, but they also work on the frontiers and peripheries of the Church's life where this tradition meets new challenges and unexplored terrain. Pope Francis has called for theologians to participate in a dialogue with science and recommended the university as a site of this encounter.[39]

Casuistry for Those Working on the Deterrent

Since Pope Francis's condemnation of deterrence, there is a need for moral theologians and philosophers, and also scholars of military and international humanitarian law, to discuss with military professionals, strategic theorists, policymakers, other professionals, and employees in the nuclear weapons field the moral issues they face in their work and to provide guidance for those currently charged with the maintenance and operation of nuclear deterrent forces. *The seventh responsibility of scholars of peace and war is to develop casuistry for those in the nuclear weapons field to help them think through the moral and ethical conflicts and choices they face in the exercise of their responsibilities within the nuclear establishment.*

John Paul II provided us with one approach to discerning these responsibilities in his encyclical *Evangelium vitae* (The Gospel of Life).[40] Pope Francis, in *Amoris laetitia* (The Joy of Love), has provided still further guidance on how to exercise this pastoral role, especially in c. 8, "Accompanying, Discerning and Integrating Difference."[41] While *Amoris laetitia* addresses issues of marital breakdown, its moral pedagogy can be applied to other difficult life situations like those now faced by men and women laboring in various ways with nuclear weapons. Scholars will need to take account of the gravity of the duties with respect to nuclear disarmament borne by those in various roles—as Finnis, Grisez, and Boyle did—including those who may continue to believe conscientiously that deterrence is morally justified.[42] They will need to address conflicts of duties and marginal situations in need of further elucidation.

Pastoral Guidance for Those Working with the Deterrent

Even as they delineate degrees of complicity with wrongful behavior in their scholarly writings, moral theologians, other pastoral workers, and just war analysts, when applying these ideas, should take into account John Paul II's pastoral principle of "gradualness," that is, "a gradualness in the prudential exercise of free acts on the part of subjects who are not in a position to understand, appreciate, or fully carry out the objective demands of the law."[43] Such caution is particularly necessary for those with an impatient sense of prophecy or an exaggerated, apocalyptic mentality about the nuclear threat.

Also, following Pope Francis's teaching, two additional principles need to be heeded: accompaniment and discernment. The Church has an obligation to accompany those faced with career changes and challenges to their professional identities from the changed moral status of nuclear deterrence in Catholic social teaching. For scholars this may involve direct engagement with nuclear specialists in conversations over how to fulfill the demands of the Church's teaching when they conflict with other responsibilities as professionals, military personnel, or patriotic citizens. In addition, even for those who dissent from the Church's teaching on deterrence, opportunities for continued participation in the life of the Church need to be affirmed in accordance with the Synod on the Family.[44]

Above all, discernment requires that moral decision-making take place in terms of the whole of a person's spiritual life.[45] As Pope Francis wrote, "There is a need 'to avoid judgments which do not take into account the complexity of various situations' and 'to be attentive, by necessity, to how people experience distress because of their condition.'"[46] Such discernment also requires attentive guidance in terms of the overall spiritual trajectory of the person's life, assessing the individual's engagement with the Gospel life, his or her development in (or loss of) Christian virtues, and the promptings of the Spirit. As Pope Francis wrote in *Amoris laetitia* with respect to divorced couples, "The Church has the responsibility of helping [workers in the nuclear field] understand the divine pedagogy of grace in their lives and offering them assistance so they can reach the fullness of God's plan for them," something that is always possible by the power of the Holy Spirit.[47] So, *the eighth recommendation is that pastoral workers applying the casuistry of the condemnation of nuclear deterrence for workers in the field ought to do so with pastoral sensitivity to the spiritual dynamics in the lives of the persons with whom they are working.*

Similarly, though scholars will need to work with conceptual precision and logical consistency in elaborating the casuistry of the abolition of nuclear weapons, *these same scholars will need to be mindful that today their casuistry will be applied in a pastoral mode*, more akin to advanced spiritual direction than to an older juridical model of confession guided by black-letter law.

Responsibilities for Just War Analysts

Just war analysts have these responsibilities:

1. Analyze deterrence within the context of a fuller ethic of peace.
2. Engage with various schools of thinking on war and peace.
3. Maintain the fire break between the casuistry of conventional and of nuclear war.
4. Incorporate the Treaty to Prohibit Nuclear Weapons and the shift in world opinion in your analyses.
5. *For moral theologians:* Help make church teaching on nuclear abolition "church-wide and parish-deep."
6. Practice just war analysis as a forensic art.

7. Develop casuistry for roles in the nuclear weapons field.
8. Apply casuistry with pastoral sensitivity.

Conclusion

I have endeavored here to provide a preliminary sketch of the responsibilities of knowledge workers in the nuclear field, taking as a starting point some guidelines for just war analysts, especially the moral theologians among them, understanding that the pastoral and academic requirements of other fields, like strategic analysts or bomb designers, will demand suitable, perhaps even distinctive, adjustment and additions to the model I have presented.

My special hope is that scholars will work together with experts, bishops, and other pastoral workers in the development of this kind of aid to implementation of the Church's teaching on the immorality of deterrence, voiced by Pope Francis on November 10, 2017. The Church works at its best when bishops and the faithful in all sectors can, in Newman's term, "conspire together" to articulate and effect its teaching on grave issues of morality.

Notes

1. Just war analysts include scholars and practitioners from an array of disciplines: theology, philosophy, international law, and military law. Here, I discuss primarily those in moral theology, particularly when I speak of collaboration with bishops and pastoral workers. Most of my recommendations, however, would hold for just war analysts from a variety of fields. I am mindful, too, that the Second Vatican Council and other church bodies have also invited the participation of people of goodwill in this kind of exercise by the Church.
2. The US bishops' 1983 pastoral *The Challenge of Peace*, after underscoring the role of conscience (nos. 231 and 280), provided general moral guidance to various classes of citizens, including pastoral workers, educators, military personnel, defense workers, scientists, and those with public responsibilities. See *The Challenge of Peace: God's Promise and Our Response*, ed. David J. O'Brien and Thomas A. Shannon (Maryknoll, NY: Orbis Books, 2010), nos. 301–29.
3. For a documentary survey of the Church's teaching and the Holy See's pronouncements on nuclear weapons, see *Nuclear Deterrence: An Ethical Perspective* (Fribourg, Switzerland: Caritas in Veritate Foundation, 2015). The collection does not include documents related to the new Treaty to Prohibit Nuclear Weapons. For them, see the documents at the Secretary of State on the Vatican website, www.vatican.va, and the documentary section of the website of the Holy See's Permanent Observer Mission to the United Nations in New York, https://holyseemission.org.
4. Pope Francis, November 10 address to this conference: "The threat of their use, as well as their very possession, is to be firmly condemned."

5. Richard Gaillardetz, "On Authority: A Short History of the Modern Magisterium," *Boston College Magazine*, Fall 2012, http://bcm.bc.edu/issues/fall_2012/c21_notes/on-authority.html.
6. On the distinction between public opinion and public judgment, see Daniel Yankelovich, *Coming to Public Judgment: Making Democracy Work in a Complex World* (Syracuse: Syracuse University Press, 1991); also see Tom Atlee, "Public Opinion, Public Judgment and Public Wisdom," http://ncdd.org/9321.
7. See Nicholas Lash, "Teaching or Commanding? When Bishops Instruct the Faithful," *America*, December 13, 2010, www.americamagazine.org/issue/759/article/teaching-or-commanding.
8. *Gaudium et spes* (Pastoral Constitution of the Church in the Modern World), no. 4, in *Catholic Social Thought: The Documentary Heritage*, ed. David J. O'Brien and Thomas A. Shannon (Maryknoll, NY: Orbis Books, 2010).
9. See Pope Paul VI, Apostolic Letter, "A Call to Action," no. 4, in *Catholic Social Thought and Pope Francis: Apostolic Exhortation, Evangelii gaudium* ("The Joy of the Gospel"), no. 51. The "communities" concerned are not just parishes but also include other groupings, like justice and peace commissions, lay religious communities, movements like Pax Christi, and communities of women and men religious. In the Church's recent pastoral theology, moreover, even the traditional parish is described as "a community of communities and movements," suggesting that subgroups within the parish may do such discernment. See, e.g., Pope Saint John Paul II's apostolic exhortation *Ecclesia in America* (Vatican City: Vatican, 1999), no. 41.
10. On the inappropriateness of the pope providing a universal response to reading of the Signs of the Times, see Pope Paul VI, *Apostolic Letter Octogesima adveniens* (A Call to Action on the Eightieth Anniversary of *Rerum novarum*), no. 4 in *Catholic Social Thought and Pope Francis, Evangelii gaudium*, no. 16. Concerning the threat of nuclear weapons, however, a strong case can be made for the importance of the pope's reading of the Signs of the Times, because it is a global problem related to the universal common good where the pope's judgment as universal pastor would be especially relevant. The papal responsibility does not relieve others, however, from the duty to discern the same issue in their own social context. The responsibility for moral discernment belongs to the whole Church.
11. On the church as a community of moral discourse, see James M. Gustafson, *The Church as Moral Decision-Maker* (Cleveland: Pilgrim Press, 1970), 81–108. An important distinction begs to be made, however, between Catholic communities of discernment and Protestant churches of a voluntary character. Catholic communities have a stronger sense of obligation to maintain the bonds of unity (communion) within the group and with the wider church through the bishops as they discern. By contrast, voluntary churches, as Niebuhr showed in his earlier book *The Social Sources of Denominationalism* (Whitefish, MT: Kessinger, 2004), tend to divide when serious differences arise among members.
12. The idea of maturation of moral judgment and of faith is inherent in Pope Francis's principle that "time is greater than space." See the apostolic exhortation *Evangelii gaudium*, nos. 6–10.

13. See Drew Christiansen, SJ, "A Conspiracy of Faithful and Bishops: Reading Newman's 'On Consulting the Faithful Today,'" *America*, September 27, 2010, www.americamagazine.org/issue/748/article/conspiracy-bishops-and-faithful. For an authoritative exposition of this teaching, see the International Theological Commission, "Theology Today: Perspective, Principles and Criteria," nos. 33–36, esp. no. 33, on the relation of bishops to the *sensus fidelium*, and Pope Francis's comments on "thinking with the Church," in "A Big Heart Open to God: The Interview," *America*, September 30, 2013, www.americamagazine.org/faith/2013/09/30/big-heart-open-god-interview-pope-francis. There, he said, "We should not even think, therefore, that 'thinking with the church' means only 'thinking with the hierarchy of the church.'"
14. For application of the expression "the long nineteenth century" to the Catholic Church's history, see John W. O'Malley, SJ, *What Happened at Vatican II* (Cambridge, MA: Harvard University Press, 2010), chap. 2, "The Long Nineteenth Century," 53–92. See Pope John XXIII, *Pacem in terris* (Peace on Earth) in *Catholic Social Thought*, nos. 148–49, on technical competence; and no. 147, on participation in public life.
15. Pope John XXIII, no. 150.
16. See *Gaudium et spes*, no. 80.
17. National Conference of Catholic Bishops, *The Challenge of Peace: God's Promise and Our Response* (Washington, DC: US Conference of Catholic Bishops, 1984), no. 320.
18. "The Harvest of Justice Is Sown in Peace: A Reflection on the Tenth Anniversary of *The Challenge of Peace*," in *Peacemaking: Moral and Policy Challenges for a New World*, ed. Gerard Powers, Drew Christiansen, SJ, and Robert T. Hennemeyer (Washington, DC: US Conference of Catholic Bishops, 1994), 333.
19. John Finnis, Germain Grisez, and Joseph Boyle, *Nuclear Deterrence, Morality, and Realism* (Oxford: Clarendon Press of Oxford University Press, 1987), 253. It should be noted that the authors' principal concern was to articulate a stronger, essentially deontological, argument against nuclear deterrence rooted in basic human goods than the consequentialist case they believed the bishops had made in *Challenge of Peace*. See pages viii and ix, 207–72.
20. On this tripartite analysis of role morality, see Dorothy Emmet, *Rules, Roles, and Relations* (New York: St. Martin's Press, 1966). I confess to not being able to identify such professional codes for scientists working in the field of nuclear weapons research. The code of the American Nuclear Society reads as a general statement of professional responsibility without specific reference to the nature of nuclear energy research or of nuclear weapons development. See www.ans.org/about/coe.
21. Pope Francis, 2017 World Day of Peace Message, "Nonviolence—A New Style of Politics for Peace," no. 6, at https://w2.vatican.va/content/francesco/en/messages/peace/documents/papa-francesco_20161208_messaggio-l-giornata-mondiale-pace-2017.html. See Pope Emeritus Benedict's discussion of *polis* in *Caritas in veritate* (Charity in Truth), no. 7, in *Catholic Social Thought*, 529. Pope Benedict's notions of the *polis* and political charity blend aspects of society and government. I do not discuss government here because it involves particular relationships and responsibilities for ethicists as advisers, consultants, etc., which are distinct, though not unrelated, to their roles as members of civil society. In addition, Pope John Paul II and the US bishops in *Challenge of Peace* locate the public debate over nuclear policy in civil society. See note 26 herein.

22. See Yoder, *When War Is Unjust: Being Honest in Just-War Thinking*, 2nd edition (Maryknoll, NY: Orbis Books, 1996).
23. On the notion of positive peace, see National Conference of Catholic Bishops, *Challenge of Peace*, nos. 68–69. The late American president John F. Kennedy, months before his death, in an address at American University, declared that peace through nuclear disarmament is "the necessary rational end of rational men." Commenting on this remark, the Vatican document "Time for Abolition" observed, "The rationality that gives rise to peace is not the technical reasoning of weapons scientists and arms control specialists. It consists rather in the broad moral reason that arises from examined living and is sourced by our historical wisdom traditions. . . . It is moral reason that tells us nuclear abolition is possible. . . . It is moral reason that recognizes that deterrence is an obstacle to peace, and leads us to seek alternative paths to a peaceful world." See "Time for Abolition," in *Nuclear Deterrence*, 92. For more on Kennedy's growing opposition to nuclear weapons, see Jeffrey Sachs, *To Move the World: JFK's Quest for Peace* (New York: Random House, 2013).
24. On integral disarmament, see Archbishop Bernardito Auza, "Statement on General and Complete Disarmament," November 16, 2017, https://holyseemission.org/contents//statements/59e52888bb4f5.php; and UN Commission on Disarmament, "Rethinking General and Complete Disarmament in the Twenty-First Century," Occasional Paper 28, October 2016, www.un-ilibrary.org/disarmament/unoda-occasional-papers-no-28-rethinking-general-and-complete-disarmament-in-the-twenty-first-century-october-2016_16471937-en.
25. See especially Carsten Stahn and Jann K. Kleffner, eds., *Jus Post Bellum: Towards a Law of Transition from Conflict to Peace* (The Hague: Asser Press, 2008).
26. On the immorality of possession, see *A Treaty to Prohibit Nuclear Weapons*, Article 1a. Also see the Holy See's contribution to the December 2014 Vienna Conference on the Impact of Nuclear Weapons, "Nuclear Deterrence: Time for Abolition," in *Nuclear Deterrence*, passim, esp. 91–92: "Now is the time to affirm not only the immorality of the use of nuclear weapons, but the immorality of their possession, thereby clearing the road to nuclear abolition."
27. *Gaudium et spes*, no. 80, in *Catholic Social Thought*.
28. On the Church's rejection of deterrence, see *Nuclear Deterrence*, passim. The UN identification number of the approved treaty text is A/CONF.229/2017/L.3/Rev.1.
29. *Nuclear Deterrence*, passim.
30. On the historic origins of the *ius gentium*, see *Natural Law: An Introduction to Legal Philosophy*, by A. P. d'Entrèves (London: Hutchinson University Library, 1951); and for a modern (liberal) approach, see John Rawls, *The Law of Peoples* (Cambridge, MA: Harvard University Press, 1999). Rawls develops his ideas out of his own political theory of justice rather than the Stoic-Christian natural law tradition, but he treats several contemporary issues, including humanitarian intervention in failed states, which was later called the Responsibility to Protect (R2P); issues of migration; and nuclear proliferation. He also condemned the 1945 atomic bombing of Japan. The International Theological Commission—in its 2009 study, "In Search of a Universal Ethic: A New Look at the Natural Law," no. 26—interestingly, speaks of the world's wisdom traditions sharing universal ethical values, especially nos. 9–20.

31. See Gerald W. Schlabach, ed., *Just Policing, Not War: An Alternative Response to World Violence* (Collegeville, MN: Liturgical Press and Michael Glazier Books, 2007), 101.
32. I refer here to the distinction made by Thomas Aquinas between the *cathedra magistralis* (the teaching authority of the professorate) and the *cathedra episcopalis* (the teaching authority of bishops).
33. See Daniel Uria, "Top Commander Would Resist 'Illegal' Nuclear Strike Order," UPI, November 19, 2017, https://upi.com/6685373.
34. See Sarah Kolinovsky, "Senate Committee Considers Trump's Authority to Launch Nuclear Weapons," ABC News, November 14, 2017, https://abcnews.go.com/US/senate-considers-trumps-authority-launch-nuclear-weapons/story?id=51139646.
35. National Conference of Catholic Bishops, *Challenge of Peace*, no. 140.
36. See Albert R. Jonsen and Stephen Toulmin, *The Abuse of Casuistry: A History of Moral Reasoning* (Berkeley: University of California Press, 1990).
37. See Vatican II, *Christus Dominus* (Decree on Bishops), no. 19.
38. Vatican II, no. 38.5.
39. *Evangelii gaudium*, nos. 133–34.
40. See Pope John Paul II, *Evangelium vitae* (Vatican City: Vatican, 1995), nos. 68–77.
41. Pope Francis, *Amoris laetitia*, nos. 291–312.
42. For a possible reading of the responsibilities of various agents, see Finnis, Grisez, and Boyle, *Nuclear Deterrence*, 342–57; and for the duties of those who continue to accept the deterrent, see 361.
43. Pope John Paul II, *Familiaris consortio*, no. 34; and see Pope Francis, *Amoris laetitia*, no. 295.
44. Pope Francis, *Amoris laetitia*, no. 299. Also see the section "The Church as Field Hospital" in the interview "A Big Heart Open to God," note 14 herein.
45. On discernment, see Pope Francis, *Amoris laetitia*, nos. 296–300.
46. Pope Francis, no. 296.
47. Pope Francis, no. 298.

26

Preliminary Conclusions

Stephen Colecchi

I have been given the daunting task of offering reflections on preliminary conclusions from this conference. I tried to listen and to learn, and will strive to present some raw material from which preliminary conclusions can be drawn. As the concept note for our gathering suggested, we are here both to "reaffirm" and to "develop" the position of the Holy See on "perspectives for a world free from nuclear weapons and for integral disarmament."

Our Holy Father, Pope Francis, repeatedly reminds us that "everything is connected." Nuclear disarmament is linked to integral disarmament, and integral disarmament is linked to integral development, and the links are reciprocal and reinforcing. Integral human development is, as Blessed Pope Paul VI taught us, "the new name for peace" (*Populorum progressio*, March 26, 1967).[1]

Everything is connected, *and* everyone is connected. National security cannot be pursued apart from collective security. Antipoverty efforts cannot be pursued apart from disarmament efforts. The arms race, including the nuclear arms race, robs humanity of the resources it needs to reduce poverty and foster integral human development. And conflict itself, with its attendant devastation, is development in reverse. Everything is connected. Everyone is connected. And these connections span to future generations as well. In a globalized age, we must see the connections and act on them.

In a sense, this is what this conference has been about. From the four corners of the world—north and south, east and west—the Holy See brought together religious leaders and representatives of civil society, officials of states and international organizations, noted academics and Nobel laureates, experts and students, to illumine the connections between nuclear disarmament and national security and between integral disarmament and integral development, and to explore the links between development, disarmament, and peace.

Prayer, spirituality, and personal encounters have infused the conference and our deliberations. Time and again, we have been reminded that in order to move toward the goal of a world free of the nuclear threat, we must free the human heart from fear and exploit the resources of hope. In this context, there have been calls for a day of prayer.

We have been blessed in a particular way to have young people among us, a reminder of the future we must shape for and with them. I am reminded of the poignant line from the message of Pope Francis to the 2014 Vienna Conference on the Humanitarian Impact of Nuclear Weapons: "Nuclear deterrence and the threat of mutually assured destruction cannot be the basis for an ethics of fraternity and peaceful coexistence among people and states. The youth of today and tomorrow deserve far more." Indeed, they do. In the words of the Holy Father, "They deserve a peaceful world order based on the unity of the human family, grounded on respect, cooperation, solidarity, and compassion."

A high point of our gathering was our audience with our Holy Father, Pope Francis. His message captured many of the themes of the conference and our discussions. I encourage all of us to read and reflect on it. Numerous times during our deliberations, we affirmed the important role of moral leaders, and particularly of Pope Francis and his predecessors.

This conference on "Perspectives for a World Free from Nuclear Weapons and for Integral Disarmament" set out to explore the links between development, peace, and disarmament. In this relatively brief time allotted to me, I am not be able to do justice to the rich tapestry of insights shared by this extraordinarily diverse and learned assembly; nevertheless, I lift up some reflections for our consideration.

Our discussions have made clear that the use and possession of nuclear weapons is prohibited. They are indiscriminate and disproportionate weapons. This would seem to suggest a shift away from an interim ethic focused on deterrence to an interim ethic focused on disarmament. In this, Pope Francis has continued the trajectory of the Church's teaching since the dawn of the nuclear age and Pope Saint John XXIII's call for a ban on nuclear weapons. We have often referred to the need to stigmatize nuclear weapons.

The dangers of nuclear proliferation in a multipolar world are evident. The more fingers that are on nuclear launch buttons, the more risks there are of a nuclear exchange. We have only to think of the current tensions between the United States and North Korea, or the long-standing tensions between India and Pakistan to find terrifying examples. To make matters worse, terrorists have no return address and cannot be deterred by the possession of nuclear weapons by others.

Nuclear deterrence is not stable. Human frailty makes it clear that mistakes and miscalculations can and do happen. Accidental launch on warning, the use of tactical nuclear weapons in response to conventional attacks, and an inadvertent escalation of crises between nuclear-possessing states are all haunting and real possibilities.

Issues of migration and its immense human costs came up several times. The vast resources spent on nuclear armaments could instead be invested in the root causes of record levels of migration. We could invest in reducing inequality and poverty, in addressing hunger and the lack of economic opportunity that drives many to migrate.

Hiroshima and Nagasaki remind humanity of what is at stake: utter destruction followed by lingering radiation. Scientists can now measure the effects of nuclear exchanges, and their findings are sobering. Everything is connected; both the human family and the common home we share will be mortally wounded, and future generations will suffer, perhaps irreparably. As we have discussed, we must disarm our hearts in order to disarm our world. The experiences of postconflict reconciliation and disarmament, and preconflict prevention, give us cause for hope.

The Treaty to Prohibit Nuclear Weapons creates a powerful international norm and is consistent with the Nuclear Non-Proliferation Treaty and the Comprehensive Test Ban Treaty. The Ban Treaty would also be complementary to a Fissile Material Cut-Off Treaty and other measures. There is a path forward for nuclear states and nonnuclear states to walk together.

Integral disarmament and integral development are connected. I loved the insight that a "world without nuclear weapons is not the present world minus nuclear weapons." In March 2017 Pope Francis wrote in a message to the UN Conference to Negotiate a Legally Binding Instrument to Prohibit Nuclear Weapons, Leading towards Their Total Elimination: "Peace must be built on justice, on integral human development, on respect for fundamental human rights, on the protection of creation, on the participation of all in public life, on trust between peoples, on the support of peaceful institutions, on access to education and health, on dialogue and solidarity." True peace is built on relationships, not armaments—least of all nuclear weapons. Nuclear weapons create a climate of fear and undermine the trust needed to build relationships. The resources wasted on nuclear armaments should be invested in a global fund to promote integral human development.

Those gathered here are idealists, but also realists. To achieve a world without nuclear weapons, rigorous verification and compliance measures will be needed, requiring global cooperation. Nuclear and nonnuclear states will need to collaborate. Structures like the International Atomic Energy Agency will be needed, and must be strengthened. Collaboration between the Church, religious communities, civil society, international organizations, and governments is essential for achieving the universal common good of a world without nuclear weapons. This will take time; it is an urgent but long-term process. Integral disarmament means that each nation's common good is connected to the universal common good. This conference has reinforced the conviction that together we can make the journey to a world without nuclear weapons.

Note

1. Pope Paul VI was canonized on October 14, 2018, almost a year after this conference.

PART VII

Closing

27

Salutations

Cardinal Peter K. A. Turkson

The Vatican's Dicastery for Promoting Integral Human Development has brought together religious leaders and representatives of civil society, officials of states and international organizations, noted academics, and Nobel laureates and students to illuminate the connections between integral disarmament and integral development, and to explore the links between development, disarmament, and peace. As our Holy Father, Pope Francis, repeatedly reminds us, "everything is connected":[1]

1. The use and possession of nuclear weapons deserve condemnation because they are indiscriminate and disproportionate instruments of war. In addressing us, Pope Francis said, "If we also take into account the risk of an accidental detonation as a result of error of any kind, the threat of their use, as well as their very possession, is to be firmly condemned."[2] Similarly reprehensible are tests of nuclear weapons and the fallout which contaminates the atmosphere and the oceans; as a global public good, their contamination could constitute crimes against humanity.
2. Nuclear deterrence does not adequately address the challenges of security in a multipolar world. In March 2017 our Holy Father wrote in a message: "If we take into consideration the principal threats to peace and security with their many dimensions in this multipolar world of the twenty-first century as—for example, terrorism, asymmetrical conflicts, cybersecurity, environmental problems, poverty—not a few doubts arise regarding the inadequacy of nuclear deterrence as an effective response to such challenges."[3]
3. Nuclear deterrence does not create a stable or secure peace; it exacerbates fear and conflict. As our Holy Father said to us: "Weapons of mass destruction, particularly nuclear weapons, create nothing but a false sense of security."[4] They also create a culture of "mutual intimidation" in the international system.
4. Spending on nuclear weapons wastes resources that are needed to address the root causes of conflicts and to promote development and peace.
5. The humanitarian effects of the use of nuclear weapons are devastating and planetary.

6. A world without nuclear weapons is possible. Pope Francis encouraged us to hope that "progress that is effective and inclusive can achieve the utopia of a world free of deadly instruments of aggression."[5]
7. Peace is built on the foundation of justice. Integral disarmament and integral development are connected. As Pope Francis recalled, Pope Paul VI "set forth the notion of integral human development and proposed it as 'the new name for peace.'"[6]
8. Nuclear disarmament is a global issue, requiring a global response. As Pope Francis wrote in March 2017: "Growing interdependence and globalization mean that any response to the threat of nuclear weapons should be collective and concerted, based on mutual trust."[7]
9. Integral disarmament is both an immediate urgent need and a long-term process. In March 2017 Pope Francis made clear: "Achieving a world without nuclear weapons involves a long-term process, based on the awareness that 'everything is connected' within the perspective of an integral ecology (cf. *Laudato si'*, 117, 138). The common destiny of mankind demands the pragmatic strengthening of dialogue and the building and consolidating of mechanisms of trust and cooperation, capable of creating the conditions for a world without nuclear weapons."[8]
10. Dialogue is essential. This dialogue must be inclusive, engaging both nuclear states and nonnuclear states, and involving civil society, international organizations, governments, and religious communities. In particular, the Catholic Church is committed to advance this dialogue at all levels.
11. Call upon states that have not yet done so, to consider signing and ratifying the Treaty on the Prohibition of Nuclear Weapons.
12. Most important, let us commit our efforts to the call for integral nuclear disarmament to prayer by all!

Everything is connected; and everyone is connected. Together, we can rid the world of nuclear weapons, invest in integral human development, and build peace. These preliminary conclusions do not represent the end of the conversation, but rather the beginning of future dialogue and action.

Notes

1. Cf. *Laudato si'*, §92.
2. "Address of His Holiness Pope Francis to Participants in the International Symposium, 'Prospects for a World Free of Nuclear Weapons and for Integral Disarmament,'" Vatican, November 10, 2017, http://w2.vatican.va/content/francesco/en/speeches/2017/november/documents/papa-francesco_20171110_convegno-disarmointegrale.html.
3. "Message of His Holiness Pope Francis to the United Nations Conference to Negotiate a Legally Binding Instrument to Prohibit Nuclear Weapons, Leading towards Their Total

Elimination," March 2017, http://w2.vatican.va/content/francesco/en/messages/pont-messages/2017/documents/papa-francesco_20170323_messaggio-onu.html.
4. "Address of His Holiness Pope Francis."
5. "Address of His Holiness Pope Francis."
6. "Address of His Holiness Pope Francis."
7. "Message of His Holiness Pope Francis."
8. "Message of His Holiness Pope Francis."

Afterword:
The Holy See and
Nuclear Disarmament—
Achievements and Challenges

Archbishop Silvano M. Tomasi

As has been clear throughout the papers included in this volume, the Holy See is a committed supporter of global nuclear disarmament and has taken concrete steps toward the achievement of this urgent objective. This afterword outlines both the considerable contributions of the Holy See and the ongoing challenges that it is seeking to address.

So far, the Holy See has made two major contributions to nuclear arms reduction, one doctrinal, the other political. Doctrinally, the Holy See has always condemned nuclear weapons as ethically unacceptable. *Jus in bello* states that the means of warfare must be proportionate and discriminate. The catastrophic humanitarian and environmental damage inflicted by nuclear weapons makes them inadmissible according to these criteria.[1] Accordingly, the Church has insisted on the need for a mutually verifiable disarmament regime and pushed for resources devoted to nuclear weapons to be channeled to promote peace and integral development.[2] Pope Francis has broken new ground in condemning nuclear deterrence. Pope Saint John Paul II for a while did judge deterrence permissible "as a step on the way toward a progressive disarmament" during the Cold War.[3] However, Pope Francis has now made the prudential moral judgment that deterrence is no longer acceptable in the current international security environment.[4] He has noted how "the principal threats to peace and security . . . in this multipolar world of the twenty-first century," are "terrorism, asymmetrical conflicts, cybersecurity, environmental problems, [and] poverty."[5] Deterrence, meanwhile "actually increases fear and undermines relationships of trust between peoples."[6]

The Holy See's significant political contribution lies in its promotion of the humanitarian initiative to abolish nuclear weapons. There has been much frustration within the international community at the failure of nuclear weapon states to comply with Article VI of the 1968 Nuclear Non-Proliferation Treaty (NPT), which provides for "a treaty on general and complete disarmament under strict and effective international control."[7]

Encouraged by Pope Francis's call for the international community to find "concrete ways to ensure that nuclear weapons are banned once and for all," an International Conference to Negotiate a Legally Binding Instrument to Prohibit Nuclear Weapons was organized in 2017, and on July 7 the parties overwhelmingly rejected the possession and use of nuclear weapons and affirmed that they are totally unacceptable.[8] The Holy See has vigorously supported the humanitarian initiative, considering it "a new hope to make decisive steps towards a world without nuclear weapons."[9] It notes how the "partnership between states, the International Committee of the Red Cross, civil society, international organizations, and the United Nations is an additional guarantee of inclusion, cooperation and solidarity," representing "a fundamental shift that meets a strong quest of a large number of the world's populations which would be the first victims of a nuclear incident."[10] Accordingly, the Holy See was the first state to become a party to the UN Nuclear Ban Treaty, signing and ratifying it on September 21, 2017.

At the same time, the Holy See supports an effective dialogue with nuclear weapon states, whose commitment remains crucial for further substantive achievements in nuclear arms control and disarmament. The Holy See can engage in this dialogue in its unique identity as a state and as a universal moral voice.

As a unique moral institution, the Catholic Church promotes a preventative culture through the concept of integral disarmament, according to which the long-term goal of abolishing nuclear weapons should be part of a broader project of developing a global ethic of peace and solidarity. This is vital for raising public awareness and creating the political will for disarmament. Especially important is the establishment of an interreligious dialogue on nuclear disarmament. As Pope Francis asserted at the 2016 Assisi World Day of Prayer for Peace, "Believers should be artisans of peace in their prayers to God and in their actions for humanity! As religious leaders, we are duty bound to be strong bridges of dialogue, creative mediators of peace."[11] By promoting interreligious dialogue on nuclear disarmament, especially with the Russian Orthodox Church, the Holy See can help to break the zero-sum ethic of security policies and replacing it with a win–win ethic of mutual goodwill.

As a state actor, the Holy See can use its diplomatic ties to facilitate dialogue and build trust between nuclear weapon countries. The first priority is to address the impending collapse of the international arms control and disarmament regime. In this difficult time for arms control and disarmament, legal obligations remain indispensable as well as dialogue among all stakeholders, to reasonably cooperate for their implementation in the pursuit of peace and stability. Furthermore, nuclear arms control and disarmament discussions could be widened to cover nonnuclear weapons systems that influence the nuclear balance of power, such as missile defense and the militarization of outer space.

The Holy See can also work multilaterally at the UN and in the other multilateral forums and advocate for the implementation of legally binding commitments assumed by nuclear weapon states signatories of the NPT, thus showing the way for other weapon states non-NPT signatories of that treaty. In the short term, the two nuclear superpowers, Russia and the United States, must resume their negotiations to reduce their arsenals to a minimum and finally do away with these weapons. If this were achieved, the remaining NPT nuclear weapon states would be more likely to agree to commit to reducing and eliminating their own arsenals on the lines of the NPT and the 2017 Treaty on the Prohibition of Nuclear Weapons. Nuclear weapon non-NPT signatories (India, Pakistan, Israel, and North Korea) would also be more inclined to accede to both treaties and to eliminate their own nuclear arsenals following the clear Russian and American examples.

More than seventy years after the first atomic bomb was dropped on Hiroshima, we should turn our thoughts to the centenary and what will have been achieved by then. Will we be living in a world free from nuclear weapons? Or will we be teetering on the brink of annihilation?

The pursuit of peace in the twenty-first century is still an elusive dream in several regions, but new technologies pose a challenge to the entire global community, and there are unknown consequences associated with nuclear weapons. The first is lethal autonomous weapons. Machines able to take human life without human control are ethically unacceptable. This is because machines will never be capable of making the judgments necessary to comply with the principles of international humanitarian law, such as distinction, proportionality, and precaution. All possible efforts must therefore be made at the United Nations to develop a treaty banning these weapons, or at the very least, to ensure a meaningful degree of human oversight.

The militarization of cyberspace also constitutes a pressing issue. Cyberattacks on critical infrastructure, such as hospitals and electrical grids, threaten the principle of distinction between combatants and noncombatants. Cyberattacks also threaten the principle of proportionality: the attacks are not violent in themselves, they simply disrupt computer operations or destroy computer data. This means that states and nonstate actors can conduct attacks with relative impunity and there are no rules governing what constitutes a proportionate response. As of yet, the UN Security Council has failed to classify any cyberactivity as a threat to or breach of the peace. However, the First Committee of the General Assembly's Group of Governmental Experts on cybersecurity may succeed in creating a consensus in this field. Significant progress has already been made; in 2015 a series of norms of cyberbehavior were issued, including the provision that states should not knowingly allow their territory to be used for internationally wrongful cyberactivities.[12] The Group of Governmental Experts' work should be encouraged in the hope that it could provide the basis for a more unified approach to cybersecurity by the Security Council.

We are still living with the consequences of the international community's failure to prohibit nuclear weapons when they were invented. It is incumbent on us to act now to prevent the proliferation of a new generation of military technologies that could prove even more insidious and lethal.

Notes

1. See "Messagio Urbi et Orbi di Sua Santità Pio XII," Easter 1958, https://w2.vatican.va/content/pius-xii/it/messages/urbi/documents/hf_p-xii_mes_19580406_urbi-easter.html.

2. See *Pacem in terris*, April 1963, http://w2.vatican.va/content/john-xxiii/en/encyclicals/documents/hf_j-xxiii_enc_11041963_pacem.html; See also *Populorum progressio*, March 1967, http://w2.vatican.va/content/paul-vi/en/encyclicals/documents/hf_p-vi_enc_26031967_populorum.html.
3. "Message of His Holiness Pope John Paul II to the General Assembly of the United Nations," June 1982, https://w2.vatican.va/content/john-paul-ii/en/speeches/1982/june/documents/hf_jp-ii_spe_19820607_disarmo-onu.html.
4. G. F. Powers, *Papal Condemnation of Nuclear Deterrence and What Is Next* (Washington, DC: Arms Control Association, 2018), https://www.armscontrol.org/act/2018-05/features/papal-condemnation-nuclear-deterrence-what-next.
5. "Message of His Holiness Pope Francis to the United Nations Conference to Negotiate a Legally Binding Instrument to Prohibit Nuclear Weapons, Leading towards Their Total Elimination," March 2017, http://w2.vatican.va/content/francesco/en/messages/pont-messages/2017/documents/papa-francesco_20170323_messaggio-onu.html.
6. "Message of His Holiness Pope Francis to the United Nations Conference."
7. "Treaty on the Non-Proliferation of Nuclear Weapons," July 1968, www.un.org/disarmament/wmd/nuclear/npt/text.
8. "Message of His Holiness Pope Francis on the Occasion of the Vienna Conference on the Humanitarian Impact of Nuclear Weapons," December 7, 2014, http://w2.vatican.va/content/francesco/en/messages/pont-messages/2014/documents/papa-francesco_20141207_messaggio-conferenza-vienna-nucleare.html.
9. "Statement by H. E. Archbishop Silvano M. Tomasi, Permanent Representative of the Holy See to the United Nations and other International Organizations in Geneva at the Vienna Conference on the Humanitarian Impact of Nuclear Weapons," December 2014, www.vatican.va/roman_curia/secretariat_state/2014/documents/rc-seg-st-20141209_tomasi-vienna_en.html.
10. "Statement by H. E. Archbishop Silvano M. Tomasi."
11. Visit of His Holiness Pope Francis to Assisi for the World Day of Prayer for Peace, "Thirst For Peace: Faiths and Cultures in Dialogue," Address of the Holy Father, September 2016, http://w2.vatican.va/content/francesco/en/speeches/2016/september/documents/papa-francesco_20160920_assisi-preghiera-pace.html.
12. L. Kello, "Cyber Threats," in *The Oxford Handbook of the United Nations*, 2nd ed., ed. T. G. Weiss and S. Daws (Oxford: Oxford University Press, 2018), 531–32.

Contributors

Alexei Georgevich Arbatov is head of the Center for International Security at the Institute of World Economy and International Relations, IMEMO, in Russia.

Monica Attias, who is based in Italy, represents the Comunità di Sant'Egidio, a worldwide Catholic organization active in caring for immigrants and refugees.

François Bugnion is a member of the Assembly of the International Committee of the Red Cross in Geneva, Switzerland.

Drew Christiansen, SJ, is Distinguished Professor of Ethics and Global Human Development in the School of Foreign Service and a senior research fellow at the Berkley Center for Religion, Peace, and World Affairs at Georgetown University in Washington, DC.

Stephen Colecchi is the former director of the Office of the International Justice and Peace for the US Conference of Catholic Bishops in Washington, DC.

Mairead Corrigan-Maguire, a Nobel Peace Prize laureate from Northern Ireland, is founder of the Community for Peace People.

Paolo Cotta-Ramusino is secretary-general of Pugwash Conferences on Science and World Affairs, which received the Nobel Peace Prize in 1995, and professor of mathematical physics at the University of Milan.

Mohamed ElBaradei is a Nobel Peace Prize laureate from Egypt, and former director-general of the International Atomic Energy Agency in Vienna.

Adolfo Pérez Esquivel is a Nobel Peace Prize laureate from Argentina.

Beatrice Fihn, who accepted the Nobel Peace Prize on behalf of the organization she founded, the International Campaign to Abolish Nuclear Weapons, is its executive director, based in Sweden.

His Holiness Pope Francis is the first pope in the nuclear era to condemn any use of nuclear weapons, classifying them instead with chemical weapons and land mines as arms that must never be used.

Rose Gottemoeller, a veteran US diplomat, is deputy secretary-general of NATO.

Thomas Hajnoczi is the permanent representative of Austria to the United Nations, based in Geneva, and director for disarmament, arms control, and nonproliferation in the Ministry for Foreign Affairs, in Vienna.

Hiromasa Ikeda is vice president of the Soka Gakkai International, a community-based Buddhist religious movement based in Japan that promotes peace, culture, and education centered on respect for the dignity of life.

Ayman Khalil is director of the Arab Institute for Security Studies, based in Jordan.

Marie-Noëlle Koyara is minister of national defense of the Central African Republic.

Emily Landau is head of the Arms Control and Regional Security Program of Israel, and senior research fellow at the Institute for National Security Studies.

Jorge Lomónaco is the permanent representative of Mexico to the United Nations in Geneva.

Monsignor Robert W. McElroy is the Roman Catholic bishop of San Diego, and a member of the Committee on International Justice and Peace of the US Conference of Catholic Bishops.

Bruno L. Müller is vice president of human resources for Mazda Motor Europe GmbH, in Germany.

Izumi Nakamitsu is the United Nations under-secretary-general and high representative for disarmament affairs.

Cardinal Pietro Parolin is secretary of state of the Holy See, in Vatican City.

Carole Sargent is the founding director of the Office of Scholarly Publications at Georgetown University and an associate of the Society of the Sacred Heart.

Susi Snyder is the primary author and coordinator of the joint PAX and ICAN project, Don't Bank on the Bomb.

Thomas Stelzer is ambassador of Austria to Portugal.

Archbishop Silvano M. Tomasi is the former permanent representative of the Holy See to the United Nations, in Geneva.

Cardinal Peter K. A. Turkson is prefect of the Dicastery for Promoting Integral Human Development, in Vatican City.

Contributors

Masako Wada is Hibakusha (a survivor of 1945 bombings in Hiroshima and Nagasaki), and assistant secretary-general of the Japan Confederation of A- and H-Bomb Sufferers Organizations, which is part of Nihon Hidankyo, a national organization of Hibakusha.

Jody Williams, a Nobel Peace Prize laureate from the United States, is chair of the Nobel Women's Initiative.

Julia Young (translator of Esquivel) is associate professor of Latin American history at the Catholic University of America.

Paul Young (translator of Koyara) is associate professor of French and Francophone studies at Georgetown University.

Muhammad Yunus, a Nobel Peace Prize laureate from Bangladesh, is the founder of the Grameen Bank.

Index

abolition, xiv–xvii, 4, 15, 22, 42–43, 51, 85–88, 113–16, 124, 126, 133n23, 145. *See also* International Campaign to Abolish Nuclear Weapons (ICAN)
accompaniment. *See* spirituality: accompaniment and direction of
Afghanistan, 23, 29
Africa, xxi, 24, 65n1, 76, 89–96, 118; Central African Republic, xxi, 89–92; South Africa, 65n1
Agenda for Sustainable Development. *See* United Nations
Amoris laetitia, 128–29, 134n41, 134nn43–47
antipersonnel mines. *See* landmines
Arab Institute for Security Studies, xxi
Arbatov, Alexei Georgevich, xx, 62–65
Arms Control and Regional Security Program, xxi, 101–3
arms trade, xx, 69
Arms Trade Treaty, 68, 70, 112
artificial intelligence, 41, 48, 64
Asia, Northeast, xx, 70, 98–99. *See also* Kim Jong Un; Korea, North; Korea, South
asymmetrical conflicts, 6, 141, 144
atomic bomb, xviii, xx, 13–16, 44, 67, 81, 83, 86, 88n1, 115, 116n1, 146
Attias, Monica, xxi, 117–19
Augustine, 125
Austria, xx, 57–58, 72

Baltic states, 62–63
Ban Treaty, xx, 7, 13, 21, 26, 45–47, 56–57, 60–61, 137, 145
Belgium, 100, 118
Benedict XVI (pope), xvi, 112, 132n21
Berio, Luciano, xx, 72
Bible, 57; Gospel, 111, 122, 129; Old Testament, 66
bomb: atomic, xviii, xx, 13–16, 44, 67, 81, 83, 86, 88n1, 115, 116n1, 146; cluster, x, 4, 27, 45–48, 87–88
Boyle, Joseph, 123, 128, 132n19, 134n42
Buddhism, xxi, 113–14
Bugnion, François, xx, 81–84

Canada, 31, 35, 104
capitalism, 29, 33, 40, 76

capital punishment, 77
Caribbean, 30–31
Caritas in veritate (papal encyclical), 132n21; Caritas in Veritate Foundation, 130
Carter administration, 121
casuistry, 123, 125, 128–30
Catholic church, xiii, xiv, xvii, 4, 57, 60, 89, 109–12, 120–34, 136–37, 142, 144; collaboration for abolition by, xix, xxii; on disarmament, 120–21; just war theory and xix, 50; peace culture and, 51; as transnational actor, xxii, 145; women of, 42
Catholic peace tradition, 124
Catholic sisters, 42–43, 88, 118, 131n9, 137, 142
Catholic Social Teaching, xvii, xxii, 4, 77, 112, 120–34, 136
CCW (Convention on Certain Conventional Weapons), 45–46
Cecil, Lord Robert, ix
CELAC. *See* Community of Latin American and Caribbean States
Central African Republic, xxi, 89–92
Challenge of Peace, The: God's Promise and Our Response, xiii–xiv, xvi, 121–22, 127, 130n2, 132n19, 132n21
chemical weapons. *See* weapons
children, 14, 17, 44, 51, 77, 86, 116–19; child soldiers, 90–91; unaccompanied minors, 117; youth, 24, 40, 50, 90, 136
China, 48, 49n1, 62–63, 65n1, 97–99, 102
Christ. *See* Jesus Christ
Christian, 4, 75, 111, 118–19, 125, 129, 133n30
Christiansen, Drew, SJ, xi, xiii–xxiii, 120–30
Churchill, Winston, 26
civil society, x, xiv–xv, xvii–xxi, 21, 32, 45–46, 57–58, 75–77, 85–88, 124
climate change, 22, 24, 32, 39
cluster munitions (bombs), x, 4, 27, 45–48, 87–88
Cluster Munitions Convention, 46, 87
Cold Start strategy, 98
Cold War, 26, 56, 62–63, 70, 73, 82, 85, 98; deterrence and, xiii, 111, 144; disarmament and, 67–69; end of, xiv, xvi, 29
Colecchi, Stephen, xxii, 135–37
common good, xv, xxi, 7, 22, 109–10, 112, 126, 128, 131n10, 137

Index

Community of Latin American and Caribbean States (CELAC), 31, 35; Havana Declaration, 31
Community of Sant'Egidio, xxi, 91, 95, 117–19
Comprehensive Nuclear Test Ban Treaty (CTBT), xx, 7, 13–14, 26, 57, 60, 68
Conference of Defense Ministers of the Americas, 31
conflict prevention, 70, 137
conflict resolution, xx, 30–35, 64, 67–68
Congress of Vienna, 23
Convention on Certain Conventional Weapons (CCW), 45–46
conversion, xi, xxi, 72, 109–12
Corker, Bob, 87
Corrigan-Maguire, Mairead, xix, 21–22, 50–52
Cotta-Ramusino, Paolo, xxi, 97–100
Crimea, xiv–xv
CTBT. *See* Comprehensive Nuclear Test Ban Treaty
Cuban Missile Crisis, ix, xiii, 44, 68, 82, 98, 123
Cummins, Bishop John S., 121
cybercrime (cyberattacks), 24, 26, 146
cybersecurity, 6, 141, 144, 147
cyberwarfare, 64, 146

DDR (disarmament, demobilization, and reintegration), 91–92
Democratic People's Republic of Korea (DPRK). *See* Kim Jong Un; Korea, North
depleted uranium. *See* uranium
deterrence. *See* Cold War; nuclear deterrence
Dicastery for Promoting Integral Human Development, x, xv, xvii, 52, 141. *See also* Vatican
dignity, 7, 14–15, 23–24, 27, 109, 114
disarmament, 4, 6, 26–27, 30–33, 42–47, 55–58, 60–61, 66–70, 72–74, 77, 81–82, 84–92, 113–14, 124–25, 128, 133n23; Catholic church and (*see* Catholic church); integral, x, xi, xv, 8, 21–22, 85, 114, 120, 125, 133n24, 135–37, 141–42, 145. *See also* abolition
disarmament, demobilization, and reintegration (DDR), 91–92
discernment. *See* spirituality: discernment of
divestment, 87–88
Donetsk, Ukraine, xv
Don't Bank on the Bomb, 87. *See also* International Campaign to Abolish Nuclear Weapons
drones, 47, 64

Ecclesia in America, 131n9
ecology, integral, xviii, 8, 142n9
economic system, xix, 39–41, 48–49, 76

Egypt, 105
Einstein, Albert, 115, 116n1
Eisenhower, Dwight, ix–x
ElBaradei, Mohamed, xxviii, 21–28, 56–57, 74, 105
elders, elderly, 14, 86, 118
encyclicals. *See Caritas in veritate; Evangelium vitae; Laudato si'; Pacem in terris; Populorum progressio*
energy, nuclear, 30, 99, 132n20
error, nuclear: detonation as a result of, xviii, xxi, 3, 97, 136; of inadvertent escalation, 98, 136; use by mistake, xviii, xxi, 3, 97–98, 136
escalation, xix, 3, 30, 32, 42, 62–64, 71
Europe, 27, 56, 62–64, 70, 76–77, 87, 118; Catholic bishops in, 42; European Union (EU), 38, 76
Evangelium vitae (papal encyclical), 128

Faith Communities Concerned about Nuclear Weapons, 114
Falkland Islands, 31
fallout. *See* radiation: fallout of
false alarms, 25–26, 97–98
Federation of Evangelical Churches in Italy, 117
Fihn, Beatrice, xix, 42–43
Finnis, John, 123, 128, 132n19, 134n42
Fissile Material Cut-Off Treaty (FMCT), xx, 22, 26, 57, 60–61, 137
food security, 48, 76, 90
France, 27, 45, 49, 97, 99, 102, 118
Francis (pope), x, xvii, 8, 17, 30, 34, 43, 46, 51–52, 57, 60, 71–72, 77, 82, 89, 112, 117, 119, 122–124, 128–29, 130n4, 131n10, 131n12, 132n13, 135–36, 141–42; *Amoris laetitia*, 128–29, 134nn41–47; condemnation of nuclear use or possession, x, xiii, xv–xviii, 3–5, 72; *Laudato si'*, xi, xviii, 8, 30, 34, 142; letter from Nobel Peace Prize laureates, 21–22; messages to the UN, 7, 66; Vienna Conference on the Humanitarian Impact of Nuclear Weapons, 110, 114; World Day of Peace Messages, 112, 132n21, 145
French Catholic Bishops Conference, 118

Gandhi, Mohandas, 17, 88
Gaudium et spes, xiii, xvi–xvii, 122–23, 126
gender, 69, 88n1. *See also* Catholic sisters; women
General Assembly. *See* United Nations
globalization, 7, 17, 22, 29–30, 33–34, 37, 72, 110, 117–18, 135, 142
global warming. *See* climate change
God, xi, xvii, 62, 72, 92, 109–10. *See also* Holy Spirit; Jesus Christ; Lord
Good Friday Agreement, 50
Gorbachev, Mikhail, xiv
Gottemoeller, Rose, xx, 55–57

Great Britain. *See* United Kingdom
Grisez, Germain, 123, 128, 132n19, 134n42
Guterres, António, 66–67, 70

Hajnoczi, Thomas, xx, 57–59
Havana Declaration, 31. *See also* Community of Latin American and Caribbean States
Hezbollah, 105
Hibakusha, xviii, 3, 13–15, 15n1, 83, 116. *See also* Hiroshima; Nagasaki
Hiroshima, xviii, xx, 3, 13, 16–17, 43–45, 51, 59, 62, 67, 81, 83, 86, 101, 136, 146; Peace Memorial Museum, 16. *See also* Hibakusha; Nagasaki
Holy See, xiv–xv, xviii–xix, xxiin8, xxiiin10, 7–8, 13, 43, 57–58, 60, 66, 82, 105, 111, 120, 130n3, 133n26, 135, 144–47. *See also* Vatican
Holy Spirit, 72, 129. *See also* God; Jesus Christ; Lord
humanitarian consequences, 26, 59, 69, 83, 101; movement, xiv–xv, xvii, xxii
humanitarian corridors, xxi, 117–19
Humanitarian Initiative, x, 4, 59–60, 81, 83, 144–45
Humanitarian Pledge, 59
Hussein, Saddam, 105
Hyten, John, 127

IAEA. *See* International Atomic Energy Agency
ICAN. *See* International Campaign to Abolish Nuclear Weapons
ICRC. *See* International Committee of the Red Cross
Ikeda, Daisaku, 113
Ikeda, Hiromasa, xxi, 113–16
immigration, 24, 90, 93. *See also* migration
inadvertent escalation. *See* error, nuclear: of inadvertent escalation
India, 49n1, 63, 65n1, 97–99, 136, 146
inequality, xiv, xv, 24, 45, 109, 136; of wealth, 24, 39–40, 136. *See also* poverty
INF. *See* Intermediate Nuclear Forces Treaty
Institute for National Security Studies (INSS) (Israel), xxi
integral disarmament. *See* disarmament: integral
integral ecology. *See* ecology, integral
Intermediate Nuclear Forces Treaty (INF), xxii, 56, 63–64, 70
International Atomic Energy Agency (IAEA), xviii, 26, 57, 74, 99, 137; LEU Bank, 26
International Campaign to Abolish Nuclear Weapons (ICAN), x, xix, 13, 32, 60, 87–88, 115; Don't Bank on the Bomb, 87
International Campaign to Ban Landmines (ICBL), 45–46. *See also* landmines

International Committee of the Red Cross (ICRC), xx, 46, 49n2, 58, 81–83, 86, 145
International Court of Justice, 26, 83
International Federation of Red Cross and Red Crescent Societies (IFRC), 81–82, 86
International Partnership for Nuclear Disarmament Verification (IPDNV), 57
international security. *See* security
International Signature Campaign in Support of the Appeal of the Hibakusha, 15
Iran, xxi, 52, 63, 70, 99, 102, 104–5
Iraq, 29
Irish Republican Army (IRA), 50–51
Islam, 99
Israel, xxi, 48, 49n1, 63, 65n1, 97, 99, 102, 104–10, 146
Italian Catholic Bishops Conference, 117
Italy, 75–76, 108, 117–20

Japan, xviii, xx, xxi, 13–17, 44–45, 51, 63, 81, 83, 99, 113–16, 133n30; Confederation of A- and H-Bomb Sufferers Organizations, xviii; Japanese Red Cross Society, 81
Jesus Christ, 109, 111–12. *See also* God; Holy Spirit; Lord
John XXIII (pope), x, xiii, xv, 4, 31, 57, 59, 77, 109–10, 123–24, 136
John Paul II (pope), xiii, xiv, xvi, 110, 124–25, 128, 144
Joint Comprehensive Plan of Action, 70, 104
Junod, Marcel, 81
just war, xix, xxii, 50, 111, 120, 123–30, 144

Kazakhstan, 26
Kehler, C. Robert, 127
Kennedy, John F., 44, 56, 113, 133n23
Khalil, Ayman, xxi, 104–6
killer robots. *See* robots
Kim Jong Un, 44, 46, 98. *See also* Asia, Northeast; Korea, North
Kissinger, Henry, xvi
knowledge workers, xxii, 120–34; professors, 120, 123, 126–34
Korea, North, 32, 44, 46, 49n1, 52, 56, 58–59, 63, 65n1, 70, 97, 99, 102, 136, 146. *See also* Asia, Northeast; Kim Jong Un
Korea, South, 48, 63, 99. *See also* Asia, Northeast
Koyara, Marie-Noëlle, xxi, 89–96

laity. *See* lay people
Lampedusa, 117
Landau, Emily, xxi, 105, 101–3
landmines, x, xix, 4, 27, 44–49; International Campaign to Ban Landmines, 45–46, 48; Mine Ban

Index

landmines (continued)
  Treaty, 45–46; Treaty to Ban Antipersonnel Landmines, 88
Latin America, 30–31
Laudato si' (papal encyclical), xi, xviii, 8, 30, 34, 142
Lawrence Livermore Laboratory, 121
lay people, 123; religious communities of, 131n9; Sant'Egidio (Catholic lay movement), xxi, 117–19
Lebanon, 117–18
LEU Bank, 26. See also International Atomic Energy Agency
Lomónaco, Jorge, xix–xx, 59–61
Lord, 4. See also God; Holy Spirit; Jesus Christ

Mahābhārata, 66
Mamberti, Dominique, xiv
Matsuda, Jujiro, 16; Matsuda family, 17
Mazda Motor Company, xviii, 16–17
Maurer, Peter, 81
McElroy, Bishop Robert W., xxi, 109–12
McNamara, Robert, 25, 98
Methodist Church. See Protestants
Mexico, xix, xx, 57
Middle East, 56, 63, 99; nuclear proliferation in, xxi, 104–6; weapons of mass destruction in, 101–3
migration, xxi, 73, 90, 117–19, 133n30, 136; immigration, 24, 90, 93; refugees, xxi, 24, 33, 90, 117–19
Mine Ban Treaty, 45–46. See also landmines
minors. See children
Minsk agreements, 64
missiles, 25, 29, 64, 88, 98, 145; ballistic, 26, 58, 65n3, 70, 97; cruise, 64; hypersonic, 64; long-range, 32, 56; medium- and short-range, 63
mistake, nuclear. See error, nuclear: use by mistake
morality, xiii, xxii, 22, 26, 47, 50–51, 60, 66, 84–85, 110, 114–16, 121, 127 136, 144–45; immorality of, nuclear weapons, x, 4, 48, 60, 130, 133n26; moral responsibilities of knowledge workers, 120–34
Mukainada spirit, 17
Müller, Bruno L., xviii, 16–17
Muslim. See Islam
Mutually Assured Destruction, xiv, 25, 86, 105, 136

Nagasaki, 3, 13–15, 44–45, 51, 59, 62, 67, 83, 101, 136. See also Hibakusha; Hiroshima
Nakamitsu, Izumi, xx, 66–72
National Conference of Catholic Bishops. See United States Conference of Catholic Bishops

NATO. See North Atlantic Treaty Organization
Newman, Cardinal John Henry, 122–23, 130, 132n13
New START Treaty, 56–57, 64, 69. See also START Treaty
Nihon Hidankyo, 13, 15
Nobel Peace Prize, x, xv, xvii, xix, xxi, 4, 13, 51, 58, 60, 74, 115; laureates, 17, 21–22, 135, 141; Women's Initiative, 48
nonnuclear states, deterrence and, xiv–xv, 137, 142n10
nonstate actors, ix, 47, 71, 98
North Atlantic Alliance / North Atlantic Council, xx, 55
North Atlantic Treaty Organization (NATO), xx, 27, 31, 55–56, 62–64, 87, 98, 100
Northeast Asia. See Asia, Northeast
Northern Ireland, xix, 50–52
North Korea. See Korea, North
Norway, 43, 57, 83
NPT. See Nuclear Non-Proliferation Treaty
NTBT. See Nuclear Test Ban Treaty
Nuclear Ban Treaty, 21, 45–47, 56–57, 60–61, 100, 137, 145
nuclear deterrence, 42, 111; abolition and, xv; casuistry and, 128; Cold War and, 111, 144; condemnation of, xvi–xvii; evolution of Catholic position on, 120–24; humanitarian consequences movement and, xiv–xv; Israel and, 105; just war and, 127; moral evaluation of, xiii–xvii; morally conditioned acceptance of, xiii–xiv; NATO and, 55; proliferation and, 25, 56; Treaty on the Prohibition of Nuclear Weapons and, 27; US-Russian relationship and, 62–64
Nuclear Disarmament: Time for Abolition, xiv–xv, 133n23, 133n26
nuclear energy, 30, 132n20
nuclear-free zones of peace. See zones of peace
Nuclear Information Resource Service, 86–87
nuclear mistake. See error, nuclear
Nuclear Non-Proliferation Treaty (NPT), xiv–xv, xvi–xviii, 7, 26–27, 30, 55–56, 58, 68–69, 84, 99–100, 104, 126, 137, 144–46
Nuclear Test Ban Treaty (NTBT), xx, 7, 13–14, 26, 57, 60, 68
nuclear-weapon-free zones, xxi, 38, 58, 104–5, 126. See also zones of peace
nuclear weapons policy, xiv, xxi, 123–25
nuclear-weapons-possessing states, xiv, xvii, xx, 136
Nunn, Sam, 25
nuns. See Catholic sisters

Oakland Diocese, 121–22
Obama, Barack, 73
Olson, Mary, 86–87, 88n1
Open Skies Treaty, 64
Organization of American States (OAS), xx, 31

Pacem in terris (papal encyclical), xi, xiii, xv, 31, 35, 57, 109–10, 112, 123
Pakistan, 45n1, 65n1, 97–99, 102, 136, 146
Paris Agreement, 39
Parolin, Cardinal Pietro, xviii, 6–9
Partial Nuclear Test Ban Treaty, 67–68
pastorality, xvi, 120–21, 126–31
pastoral letters of the US bishops: *The Challenge of Peace*, xiii, xvi, 122–23, 130n2; *The Harvest of Justice is Sown in Peace*, xvi, xxii, 123, 132n18
Paul VI (pope), 4, 8, 122–23, 135, 137n1, 142
PAX, xx
peacekeeping, xxi, 24, 64, 90–92
peacemaking (peacemakers), x, xxi, 15, 124, 132n18
peace tradition. *See* Catholic peace tradition
Pecorario, Alessio, 120
Pérez Esquivel, Adolfo, xix, 21–22, 29–37
Perry, William, 25
Petrov, Stanislav, 97–98
PoA (Programme of Action to Prevent, Combat, and Eradicate the Illicit Trade in Small Arms and Light Weapons in All Its Aspects), 69
Pontifical Council for Justice and Peace, ix. *See also* Vatican
poor. *See* poverty
popes. *See specific popes by name*
Populorum progressio (papal encyclical), 4, 8, 75, 135
Portugal, xx, 73
poverty, xv, xix, 3, 6, 8, 23–24, 27, 39, 51, 73, 90, 112, 135–36, 141n2, 144. *See also* wealth inequality
prayer, xvii, 15, 43, 109, 135, 142, 145
professors. *See* knowledge workers: professors
Programme of Action to Prevent, Combat, and Eradicate the Illicit Trade in Small Arms and Light Weapons in All Its Aspects (PoA), 69
prohibited weapons. *See* weapons
Protestants, x, 4, 131n11; Federation of Evangelical Churches in Italy, 117; Methodist Churches, 117; Protestant Churches of France, 118
Pugwash Conferences on Science and World Affairs, xxi

R2P (Responsibility to Protect), 133n30
radiation, 15, 83, 86–87, 88n1, 136; fallout of, 83
rationality, 59, 73, 133n23; rational end of rational men, 133n23
rationalization, 120, 125
Rawls, John, 133n30
Reagan, Ronald, xiv, xxii, 64–65; administration of, 121
Red Crescent Movement, 81–82, 86. *See also* International Federation of Red Cross and Red Crescent Societies
Red Cross. *See* International Committee of the Red Cross (ICRC)
refugees. *See* migration: refugees
repression, 24
Responsibility to Protect (R2P), 133n30
Rio+20, 74, 76
robots, 76, 48; killer, 44, 47–48, 76
Russia, xiv–xv, xx, 26, 48–49, 62–65, 97–99, 145–46. *See also* Cold War
Russian Federation, 56–57
Russian Orthodox Church, 145

Saudi Arabia, 63, 99
Schengen area, 118
Schlabach, Gerald, 126
scholars. *See* knowledge workers
Second Vatican Council, xiii, xvi–xvii, 122–23, 126–28, 130n1
security, ix–xx, 6–8, 22–28, 30–31, 46–47, 55–59, 65–71, 74, 82, 99, 103–4, 111, 114, 116, 118–19, 126, 135, 141, 144–46; cyber (*see* cybersecurity); false sense of, xv, xxii, 3, 6; food (*see* food security); norms, 7, 66, 68–70, 75, 101–3, 111, 124–25, 127
Security Council. *See* United Nations
SGI (Soka Gakkai International), xxi, 113–16
Shultz, George P., xvi
signs of the times, ix, 122, 131n10
Sinai, 105
Snyder, Susi, xx, 85–88
Soka Gakkai International (SGI), xxi, 113–16
South Africa, 65n1
South America, 31; South American Commission for Peace, Regional Security, and Democracy, 31
South Korea. *See* Korea, South
Soviet Union. *See* Russia
spirituality, 51, 84, 109, 113, 123, 129, 135; accompaniment and direction of, x, xvii, 120, 127, 129; discernment of, ix, x, xvii, 122–23, 127–29, 129, 131nn9–11, 134n45
Stalin, Joseph, ix
START Treaty, xxiin6, 56, 64; New START Treaty, 56–57, 64, 69

Stelzer, Thomas, xx, 72–77
Stevenson, Adlai, 23
Stoltenberg, Jens, 56
Strategic Air Command, xvii, 127
students, 135, 141
superpowers, xvi, 63–64, 99, 145
sustainable development, 8, 39, 68, 70–71, 73, 76, 88
Sustainable Development Goals. *See* United Nations: sustainable development
Syria, 23, 103, 117–18; Syrian Civil War, 24

terrorism (terrorists), 4, 6, 22–25, 47, 63, 68, 98–99, 111, 119, 136, 141, 144
Test Ban Treaty. *See* Nuclear Test Ban Treaty (NTBT)
Thurlow, Setsuko, 43, 85–86
Tomasi, Archbishop Silvano, xi, xiv, xxii, 144–46
TPNW. *See* Treaty on the Prohibition of Nuclear Weapons
Treaty of Tlatelolco (Treaty for the Prohibition of Nuclear Arms in Latin America and the Caribbean), 30, 34
Treaty on Conventional Forces in Europe, 70
Treaty on the Prohibition of Nuclear Weapons (TPNW), x, xv, xvi, 7, 13, 15, 26–27, 57–59, 82–84, 86–87, 113–15, 120, 125–26, 130n3, 137, 142
Treaty to Ban Antipersonnel Landmines, 88. *See also* landmines
Truman, Harry, 43
Trump, Donald, 98; president's sole authority to launch nuclear weapons, 127, 134n34
Turkey, 63, 81, 100
Turkson, Cardinal Peter, ix–xi, xv, xvii, xxii, 3, 72, 141–43

UK. *See* United Kingdom
Ukraine, xiv, 62–64; Donetsk region of, xv
Union of South American Nations, 31
United Kingdom, 27, 31, 49–50, 97, 99, 102, 104
United Nations, ix–xx, xxiin4, 6, 15, 21, 23, 25, 32, 55, 57–60, 66–67, 70, 72–75, 82, 88n1, 91, 94–95, 99, 104, 111, 114, 126, 146, 147n3; Conference to Negotiate a Legally Binding Instrument to Prohibit Nuclear Weapons, 5–6, 9n1, 55, 57–58, 137, 142n3, 145; sustainable development, 6, 8, 39, 51, 68, 70–71, 73, 76, 88
unaccompanied minors. *See* children
United States, xx, 13, 26–27, 31–32, 52–53, 44–47, 62–65, 65n3

United States Conference of Catholic Bishops, ix, xiii, xiv, xvi, 42, 121–23, 125–26, 127–28, 130, 130nn1–2, 131n7, 131n11, 132n13, 132nn17–18, 132n21, 133n23
uranium, 26, 29, 33
utopia, 4, 6, 8, 47–48, 67, 142

Vatican, xiv, xv–xviii, 15, 23, 47, 55, 57–58, 60, 66, 81, 84, 89, 93, 105, 111, 120, 124, 130n3, 133n23, 135, 142–43n3, 146n1; Dicastery for Promoting Integral Human Development, x, xv, xvii, 52, 141; Pontifical Council for Justice and Peace, ix. *See also* Holy See
Vatican Council II. *See* Second Vatican Council
Vienna Conference on the Humanitarian Impact of Nuclear Weapons, xiv, xxiiinn10–11, 83, 110, 114, 133n26, 136, 147nn8–9
Vienna, Congress of, 23
Vienna Document, 64

Wada, Masako, xviii, 13–15
Waldensians, 117
warfare, x, xix, 4, 22, 31, 64–65, 67, 82–83, 125, 144, 146
wealth inequality, 24, 39–40, 136. *See also* poverty
weapons, x, xix, xvi, 4, 7, 22, 27, 45–47, 64, 67, 68–69, 82, 87, 89, 91–92, 100, 136, 145–46, 149
Weapons of Mass Destruction (WMD), ix–x, 3, 7, 24, 27, 32, 38, 42, 45, 58, 67, 86, 101–3, 141
Williams, Jody, xix, 21–22, 44–49, 73
women, xix, 39, 42, 48, 50–51, 86, 90, 118. *See also* Catholic sisters; gender
Women's Initiative, Nobel. *See* Nobel Peace Prize: Women's Initiative
women's religious congregations. *See* Catholic sisters
World Day of Peace Messages, 112, 132n21, 145. *See also* Francis (pope)
World Social Forum, 31
World War II, ix, 13–16, 44–45, 51, 67, 83, 104–5

Yeltsin, Boris, 98
Yoder, John Howard, 124, 133n22
youth. *See* children
Yugoslavia, former, 29, 33
Yunus, Muhammad, xix, 21–22, 38–41, 44, 48, 76

zones of peace, 30–31. *See also* nuclear-weapon-free zones

www.ingramcontent.com/pod-product-compliance
Lightning Source LLC
Chambersburg PA
CBHW031447160426
43195CB00010BB/886